Breaking the Bread of Revelation
Volume 1

Breaking the Bread of Revelation

Volume 1

Brian McCallum

Brian McCallum Ministries
12645 East 127th Street South
Broken Arrow, OK 74011

Unless otherwise indicated, all scriptural quotations are from the
King James Version of the Bible.

Breaking the Bread of Revelation, Volume 1
Published by:
Brian McCallum Ministries
12645 E. 127th St.
Broken Arrow, OK 74011
ISBN 0-962-0883-0-7

Tenth Printing, July 2010

Cover design and book production by:
Double Blessing Productions, Inc.
P.O. Box 52756, Tulsa, OK 74152
www.doubleblessing.com

Editorial Consultant: Phyllis Mackall, Broken Arrow, Oklahoma

Printed in the United States of America.

Contents

Author's Preface

Thirty-seven percent of our Bible is made up of prophecy. If this much of the Bible contains prophecy, we need to have a proper understanding of what prophecy is. It would be difficult to remove thirty-seven percent of your Bible and be able to understand the remainder of it.

This book will be a study of Bible prophecy. We will concentrate on the Book of Revelation, but we will also consider Old and New Testament scriptures that verify what the Book of Revelation says.

No Private Interpretation

There is no better way to understand the Word of God than by what the Word says about itself. No private interpretation of scripture works. One reason why there are so many different opinions regarding end-time prophecies is because people have developed so many private interpretations of scripture.

Frankly, the different ways that people imagine Jesus will come again wouldn't exist if there hadn't been a great deal of private interpretation of God's Word. But Jesus is not coming again in ten different ways — or even five, three, or two different ways!

Jesus is returning just one way — just as He came one way the first time. And I firmly believe that God

i

has shown us in His Word how Jesus' Second Coming is going to happen.

I also believe that we can know exactly *how* He is really returning if we will study the Book of Revelation "to show ourselves approved." We should study this book the same way we study any other part of the Word of God, by relying on the Holy Spirit — the Author.

Some may argue, "Well, why don't you teach the different ways that people believe Jesus will return?" My answer is that these theories rely on head (natural) knowledge. Studying them would mean we were leaning on our own understanding — and you wouldn't be any more enlightened about the matter after studying them than you were when you started.

In fact, studying all these opinions of men would only serve to confuse you — and they could hinder your grasping the great spiritual truths God has for you in this study.

Therefore, I'm going to teach you what the Word of God itself says, and you may then draw your own conclusion. This is the only safe way to draw a conclusion: seeing the Word agree with itself.

Furthermore, Bible prophecy is not a subject one can skim over lightly to come to an accurate judgment about what is going to happen in history.

The Harmony of the Epistles

Another objective of our study will be to recognize the harmony between the Book of Revelation and other New Testament epistles. Revelation actually is an *epistle* written to the Church. Perhaps it is not often considered an epistle, but that's what it actually is. Also, Revelation was not written *before* the Church Age; it was written *in* the Church Age — for a reason.

Readers of the Book of Revelation must be able to put themselves in the place of a first-century believer in order to fully understand this book. That's why the book wasn't given before the Church Age: It is the completion and fulfillment of all that the prophets said. And in our study of Revelation, we will see that completion and fulfillment.

Throughout the Book of Revelation we will observe the revelation of Jesus Christ — because that's what the Book of Revelation is: the revelation of Jesus!

As we study the Book of Revelation, we will learn more about *the grace of God.* Most people don't think of Revelation as a book that reveals God's grace, but notice at the very beginning, John writes, "John to the seven churches which are in Asia: *Grace be unto you, and peace,* from him which is, and which was, and which is to come. . ." (Revelation 1:4). You will find that this pattern is consistent throughout the majority of New Testament epistles.

Peace: An Unexpected Blessing

John wrote this epistle under the unction of the Holy Spirit in order to extend grace and peace to believers. If you're going to receive grace and peace from reading Revelation, you won't be biting your fingernails in distress when you finish it, will you?

John didn't expect you to dig a deep hole in your backyard to hide in when all the events outlined in Revelation begin to happen. Neither did he expect you to store up food, water, and survival gear, making *natural* preparations for *supernatural* happenings.

After reading the Book of Revelation, you will be at peace about the future, because that's what the Word communicates: grace and peace!

Paul writes to Timothy, "Thou therefore, my son, be strong in the grace that is in Christ Jesus. And the things that thou hast heard of me among many witnesses, the same commit thou to faithful men, who shall be able to teach others also" (2 Timothy 2:1,2).

Ditches To Avoid

In the present hour, the enemy is working hard to distract Christians from their task. If you are going down the middle of the road in your Christian walk, you will feel one force trying to pull you to the right and another force trying to pull you to the left. Both are trying to get you into a ditch!

Believers need to stay in the middle of the road. No one knows *everything* about the end times, but there is a middle path — a path of moderation — to be found in the Word of God.

One "ditch" that Christians often fall into is the erroneous belief that *the Church* was commissioned to turn the world into paradise before Jesus comes. That is not true. When Jesus returns, *He* will do that. He will use you to help Him, but He is the One who is going to create a perfect society and world.

Until Jesus comes, the Church does have a task He gave us to do: to preach the Gospel to every creature on the face of this earth and to take out of the kingdoms of this world all that belongs to God — the harvest of souls which Jesus' blood purchased!

When Jesus gave the Great Commission to the Church, He didn't say, "Go ye into all the world and turn it into paradise." He didn't say, "Go and correct everything that's wrong." What He said was, "Go preach the Gospel. Proclaim the Good News." And when the Church is finished doing that, He said He'd come again and gather us unto Himself.

There are some people — especially faith people — who are susceptible to believing that the task of the Church is to turn the world into a paradise before Jesus returns. Because they fully understand the power of confession, it is easy for them to be drawn a little beyond what the Word says.

The Word does not say that Christians are going to turn the world into a paradise before Jesus comes. The Word says that if Christians will preach the Gospel in every nation, then Jesus will come again. *The only reason why Jesus hasn't returned is because we haven't fulfilled His Great Commission yet!*

In First Thessalonians, Paul writes about Christ's Second Coming, and in the fourth chapter he concludes, "Wherefore comfort one another with these words" (v. 18). Whenever Paul teaches about the end times, he doesn't leave us in a quandary; he gives us *comfort!*

The Conspiracy Theory

The exact opposite of Paul's emphasis is happening today. Well-known speakers are going from church to church, getting believers so nervous about the future that they don't know what to do. These speakers imagine a great *conspiracy.* They convince their audiences that the devil is just about to take over the whole world and destroy the Church. That's the other ditch!

Stay in the middle of the road. Don't get off on either of these tangents. *"Comfort one another* with these words." Keep in mind what Paul said in First Thessalonians 5:11, *"Wherefore comfort yourselves* together, and *edify one another,* even as also ye do."

Whatever we learn about the end times should be *comforting* to us. It should be *edifying* to us. It should *build us up*. And it should communicate *grace* to the hearers. Grace!

Brian K. McCollum

Chapter 1
Introduction to Revelation

The Book of Revelation is not some weird book that was tacked onto the end of the Bible so everyone can wonder what it's all about!

The Book of Revelation is part of the revelation or mystery God has given to us because we are in the kingdom of heaven.

Notice that the book begins with the words, "The Revelation of Jesus Christ...." This revelation is not *from* Jesus, or *by* Him, but *of* Him.

The Book of Revelation, then, is going to reveal Jesus Christ to us: "The Revelation of Jesus Christ, which God gave unto him, to shew unto his servants things which must shortly come to pass...." Not to hide from; to show unto his servants.

Are you one of God's servants? If you have become one, you are qualified to receive this revelation, because you are a member of Christ's Body.

God wants you to know about the things He's going to do in the earth. He doesn't want to keep the knowledge of these events from you; He wants you to be aware of what's coming in the future. And God has given us the means to know these "...things which must shortly come to pass; and he sent and *signified* it by his angel unto his servant John" (Revelation 1:1).

1

Symbolism in Revelation

"Signified" is an important word. It means that God made a *symbolic* presentation, primarily, in the Book of Revelation. In other words, what God shows us in this book was written, for the most part, in symbolic form. And because this is so, we will need to interpret a number of symbols in order to understand the book.

However, we won't be able to understand Revelation by any private interpretation. We won't be able to get by with saying, "Well, this *sounds like* that," or "John must have seen this and *thought* it was that, because he didn't know what it was." Such speculations originate from your mind, or the natural realm, and they won't get you anywhere in the spiritual realm.

The Bible will interpret the Bible, because it agrees with itself — and this holds true of the Book of Revelation as well as any other book. You will find agreement throughout the Bible, from Genesis to Revelation.

Do you own a signet, or class ring, from your high school or college? Mine has the words "Rhema Bible Training Center" encircling it, plus the year that I graduated, the word "faith," and a cross with the word *rhema*. If you took that ring and dipped its crest into wax placed on a piece of paper, it would leave an imprint or sign, wouldn't it? It would *signify* that it was a Rhema ring.

Men in past centuries commissioned jewelers to create ornate seals to identify themselves. When they sent a letter or other document to someone, they would dip their signet into the wax, which then sealed the document. If the seal was still unbroken when the document was delivered, the recipient would know that no one had tampered with it or read it; resealing was so obvious.

Only one man would own a particular signet, and he would always use it to symbolize himself in his correspondence. It stood for him.

What we are about to find in the Word of God is similar to this practice. We are going to learn many symbols that stand for something else. Bear in mind that the man is not his ring; the ring *stands for* him. We'll see many things in this Book of Revelation that are like that. They're not understood in themselves; they stand for something else, and you must understand what it is.

Influences From the Past

It will be difficult not to depend upon what you've already heard, learned, and understood about the Book of Revelation. If you have read a great deal about end-time prophecy, that information will also stick in your mind.

After I became born again about twenty-four years ago, the first topic I wanted to study was what was going to happen at the end of time. I believe many new believers are like that — but that is the last topic new believers need to be interested in! (For one thing, they should be interested in finding out who they are in Christ.)

So, as a young Christian, I read a number of books about the end times — and I became thoroughly confused. Every author had a different viewpoint! Some thought we were going to live through the Great Tribulation. Others thought that the Church would be battered, smashed, and tramped on by the anti-Christ. Still others thought that just before the wrath of the anti-Christ got too terrible to bear, the Church would escape (but barely). These are just a few of the opinions I discovered.

After reading all those books on eschatology, it was difficult for me to look into the Word objectively, without being influenced by what I had read.

I would like to suggest that before we begin this study, you try to clear your mind, to the best of your ability, of all your previously held beliefs about the Book of Revelation. Instead, concentrate on understanding *precisely what the Word says.*

I am not asking you to believe everything in Revelation exactly the way I do; I am simply asking you not to deny what you may see in the Word of God. Allow the Spirit of God to minister these truths from Revelation to your heart. As you keep an open mind, I believe you will see clearly what God wants you to see in the Book of Revelation.

Also, all of us are in the process of learning the depths of the treasures found in God's Word. No one knows everything, and no one should claim to. I don't claim to be one hundred percent accurate about everything I currently understand about this book; however, I am striving to come to a place of mastery in my investigation.

Let us all trust God to show us what He wants us to see in these scriptures. He inspired the Apostle John to write this material for a reason — and it was not to confuse us. After all, God is not the author of confusion!

"He Will Show You Things To Come"

In John 16:13, we read, "Howbeit when he, *the Spirit of truth,* is come, he will guide you into all truth...and he will shew you things to come."

4

Now turn to Revelation 19:10, where John writes, "And I fell at his feet to worship him. And he said unto me, See thou do it not: I am thy fellowservant, and of thy brethren that have the testimony of Jesus: worship God: for the testimony of Jesus is *the spirit of prophecy.*"

The spirit of truth and the spirit of prophecy are not two different spirits; they're the same Holy Spirit. The testimony of Jesus Christ is the spirit of prophecy. He is the Word of God, isn't He?

So prophecy is not something weird or difficult to understand. Prophecy in this sense is simply what God would have you know about things that are going to happen in the future. Remember, Jesus said He would show His friends things that were to come (John 16:13,14). And you are His friends!

Jesus is not hiding truths about the end times from you. He simply stated these truths symbolically in Revelation so that the world wouldn't understand them — so that people who are just intellectually curious, or who don't care, or who would misuse the knowledge, won't know about matters He doesn't want them to know.

But Jesus does want *you* to know about the end times, and He has made this information available in the Book of Revelation to all who belong to Him.

The testimony of Jesus is the spirit of prophecy. As we read the Book of Revelation, whom will we see as its main character? *Jesus Christ,* not the anti-Christ!

We will not concentrate our studies on the Tribulation, the false prophet, or other unusual topics. It is Jesus Christ whom we will see fulfilled and completed in Revelation: He is the main character all the way through the book.

5

Listen to the Author

We saw in John 16 that when the spirit of truth — the Holy Spirit — is come, He will guide you into all truth. *All truth*, not just some truth, "...for he shall not speak of himself; but whatsoever he shall hear, that shall he speak: and he will shew you things to come."

One way (not the only way) the Holy Spirit shows you things to come is by giving you light on the prophetic word. Jesus said, "...the words that I speak unto you, they are *spirit*, and they are *life*" (John 6:63). All the words Jesus ever spoke have to be like this, don't they? This would include the words Jesus prophesied concerning the future. (Prophecy about the future is not confined to the Old Testament prophets or to the apostles. Jesus Himself prophesied about the future.)

As we saw, another way Jesus shows us things to come is by giving us light on His prophetic word. Do we get it when we're asleep, or meditating quietly? Although God often does speak to us out of our hearts while we're meditating or sleeping, Second Timothy 2:15 gives us a clearer instruction: "*Study* to shew thyself approved unto God, a workman that needeth not to be ashamed, rightly dividing the word of truth."

To "rightly divide," we've got to have help from the Holy Spirit, don't we? He will lead and guide us into all truth, and He will show us things to come.

Lean upon the Holy Spirit to show you the truth. You know God gave you a mind to use, don't you? But don't lean solely upon your intellect for understanding of spiritual matters. Lean upon the Spirit of God to show you the truth. He'll enlighten your mind, because the Word renews the mind.

It's not the other way around: The mind doesn't interpret the Word; your heart does. Use your heart to do it. Allow the Holy Spirit, who is dwelling in your spirit, to lead you in this quest.

What should you do if you start reading something that doesn't agree with what you've heard before: Reject it immediately? Say, "Oh, no, that can't be right"? No! Just relax and let God minister to you from His Word. Listen to what the Word says, because the Word will tell you what is true.

The same holds true for understanding prophetic scriptures. Listen to what the Word says to you after you've studied it. It's your responsibility to study the Bible. If you don't, how can you expect to understand major issues correctly?

You can't depend totally upon someone else's study, either. What an author learned may not be everything *you* need to know. What he or she saw is not necessarily all there is to understand about a certain subject; his viewpoint only represents what God has shown to one person — and we all see in part. The Bible is the revealed Word of God. As you study it, you'll discover more and more truth.

How To Study the Word of God

A good principle to follow is this: Always take the "plain sense" (or obvious meaning) of a scripture to mean exactly what it says.

In this book, when a verse makes plain sense, we'll take that plain sense meaning. In fact, we won't ignore the plain sense of a passage even when we are examining symbols. However, we will study the symbols found in the Book of Revelation, because we can learn a great deal from them.

Symbols are used in a consistent manner throughout the Word of God. If God uses a symbol to represent

Jesus Christ in one book, that same symbol will represent Him in another book. God doesn't use one symbol to represent both Jesus Christ and the anti-Christ. God is not only consistent; He doesn't lack for symbols to use.

This is an important clue in the interpretation of symbols: Find the symbolic use elsewhere in the Word and note the consistency of its use.

For example, take a good concordance and look up the word "white." See what it symbolizes. You'll find that it is used consistently, from Genesis to Revelation, to symbolize such aspects of God's character as purity, righteousness, justice, and holiness. It *always* symbolizes these things.

When you reach the Book of Revelation, you can rest assured that the color white does not suddenly represent something totally different, like the devil or the anti-Christ. It never does.

Knowing this should help you. Again, look for the consistent use of symbolic words, and you'll be able to understand what is meant in different passages.

When There Is No Obvious Meaning

Of course, there are some passages where there is no obvious meaning, because God is deliberately using symbols to convey the meaning.

An example of this is found in the ninth chapter of Revelation: "And the fifth angel sounded, and I saw a star fall from heaven unto the earth: and to him was given the key of the bottomless pit" (v. 1).

This is the time when the trumpets are sounding in the time of the Great Tribulation. There is a great deal of symbolic language in this statement. John didn't attempt to state this in such a way that you would derive an obvious meaning from it.

The "star" that fell from heaven to earth is not a literal star. It's not one of the stars you see when you look up into the heavens at night.

How do I know? It's very simple: If a literal star fell out of its place in the heavens, it would destroy the earth! Stars are bigger than the earth; even the smallest star is bigger than the earth. It's like comparing a huge beach ball to a tiny pea. And a star is a big mass of hot gas. When it reached the earth's atmosphere, the star would not be destroyed; instead, it would burn up the earth's atmosphere and then the earth itself. So you can't make plain sense out of such a verse.

What does a star symbolize? An angel! Over and over again, from Genesis to Revelation, God has used the word "star" to symbolize angels.

Now let's examine the verse even more closely. It says that a star fell and "to *him*" was given the key to control the bottomless pit, which is something like an abyss under the earth, a part of Hades. From this example you can see that you must know what symbolic language means in order to understand such a verse.

A good study method is to always look first for the plain sense in a verse. But don't quit there; also look for the symbolic sense, because all verses do not make plain sense. *Most prophecy contains both plain sense and symbolism.*

Layers of Meaning

The Book of Revelation is composed of overlaying levels (or layers) of meaning. John will discuss a certain subject for a while; then he will switch to another subject. Afterwards, he will return to his first subject.

This is a similar style to the first two chapters of Genesis. In the first chapter, God gives us an account of creation. In the second, He gives us more details about creation — and this is how much of Revelation was written.

The Book of Revelation was not written in chronological order! The events of chapter 13 do not necessarily follow chapter five — and chapter five doesn't necessarily happen chronologically after chapter four. (Chapter 13, however, is an overview of what John already said in chapter eight. He just gives more details about it.)

We will study enough of Revelation to understand principles of interpretation, plus some of that interpretation itself. Of course, it will be impossible to interpret the entire book in this volume. We can't even come close. But we will spend enough time in certain areas to enable you to understand how to interpret Revelation for yourself.

Chapter 2
Beginning Our Study

Looking again at the opening verse of the book, we see that "The revelation of Jesus Christ" is a revelation of Jesus which God gave "unto him, to shew unto his servants things which must shortly come to pass."

Now look at the phrase "shortly come to pass." Remember, God sent this revelation through the Apostle Paul in the first century. Those things were *already* happening then, and some of them are *still* happening today.

To us, that time span — approximately two thousand years — is a long time; but to God, it is only "shortly." Many things are stated like that in Revelation. You must understand that God is stating this from His point of view, not from ours.

People stumble over some things that God has said because they haven't happened yet. As the apostles predicted, some people complain, "Why hasn't God done what He said He was going to do? He said it a long time ago. Why hasn't He done it?"

The fact that some things have not happened yet does not mean that God is *not* going to fulfill His promises! For example, God said He would send a Savior four thousand years before Jesus came! And God kept repeating His promise during those four thousand years. Jesus Christ finally came when man was able to believe and obey God to the degree necessary to bring Him forth. God *did* keep His word to mankind: Jesus *did* come!

Seeing Revelation From God's Perspective

Therefore, it is important to view the Revelation of Jesus Christ from God's perspective. The entire first verse of Revelation 1 reads: "The Revelation of Jesus Christ, which God gave unto him, to shew unto his servants things which must shortly come to pass; and he sent and signified it by his angel unto his servant John."

Remember, we said "signified" shows us the symbolic content of this book. God has greatly symbolized this revelation so that those who understand these symbols will be able to understand the book, and those who don't, won't.

Now let us look at verse two: "Who bare record of the word of God, and of the testimony of Jesus Christ, and of all things that he [John] saw."

We learned earlier in the nineteenth chapter that the testimony of Jesus is the spirit of prophecy. *There is no spirit of prophecy that concentrates on the negative,* even though you will hear so-called prophets today concentrating on the negative, saying how terrible things are going to get in the future.

But the spirit of prophecy is the testimony of Jesus Christ! That doesn't mean that Revelation doesn't *include* negative things, because it does. The things John saw weren't all pleasant, but John doesn't *emphasize* or dwell on them.

12

Verse 3: "Blessed is he that readeth, and they that hear the words of this prophecy, and keep those things which are written therein: for the time is at hand."

Again, it's "near at hand." It was already happening, and it is continuing to happen. Nineteen hundred years ago, John wrote that his age was a time when many of those things were being fulfilled. And they're still being fulfilled today: We're seeing some of them fulfilled before our very eyes!

The Pressure of Current Events

But that poses a problem. People who teach prophecy are always pressured to match current events with Bible prophecy; particularly prophecy in the Book of Revelation. Every time a crisis happens in the world, people want an explanation from the Bible.

When Israel invaded Lebanon, my students came running to me, asking, "Where's that in the Bible?" They were disappointed when I replied, "I don't know; I can't find it in the Bible."

But the pressure is there, and in such cases, someone will usually find an obscure scripture that mentions Lebanon and proclaim, "This must be it!" Then they and their followers will plunge into some ditch.

That's not the way to interpret the Bible. Don't interpret the Bible from what happens in the world. You don't interpret the rest of it that way, do you? Yet many sincere Christians have been destroyed because they did exactly that. They interpreted the Bible from things that happened to them in their own life.

If they didn't get healed, they thought, "I'll find a scripture that will tell me why I didn't." And they found Job or someone like him and justified themselves instead of justifying God.

So don't use what happens in the world to interpret what you read in the Word. Do it the other way around: Know the Word so well that when the things the Word is talking about occur, you'll know they're occurring.

Everything that happens in the world is not found in the Bible. On the other hand, some things that happen in the world are found in the Bible.

Did you ever study world history? You have probably noticed by now that some of the people you studied in secular history are also found in the Bible — but not *all* the famous people in secular history are found in the Bible; just certain ones. Which ones? The ones who affected the Redemption of mankind. The ones whom God used. The ones who had a part to play in God's plan for the ages.

For example, consider Cyrus, the king of Persia. God mentioned him in scripture even before he was born. God said Cyrus would set the Jews free from their Babylonian captivity when it was time for them to leave. There were many Persian kings who ruled that ancient nation, but you won't find their names in the Bible. Cyrus played a part in God's plans, so he is found in the Bible.

Do not try to relate everything that happens today in the Middle East to some passage in the Bible, because *everything* that happens there is *not* in the Bible. Many prophecy teachers fall into that trap. Because prophecy is their specialty, they think they *need* to comment on every event. That's not right.

"Blessed is he that readeth, and they that hear the words of this prophecy, and keep those things which are written therein . . ." (Revelation 1:3). In other words, we are to be doers of the Word; we are to do what God tells us in His Word.

The Entire Church for the Entire Age

In the next passage, God will tell you what it is He wants you to have: grace and peace for living today. Verse 4 begins, "John to the seven churches which are in Asia . . . ."

So if you read the Book of Revelation and you get nervous about what's coming in the future, you haven't understood the message of the book. Or if you listen to someone teaching on the Book of Revelation and you end up in a quandary, you still haven't heard it. What is this message? John says his message is, "*Grace* be unto you, and *peace* . . . ."

If you have an accurate understanding about what will happen in the future, you won't be overly concerned. I don't mean you won't care about it; I mean you won't concentrate on the *future*. Instead, you'll concentrate on the *present*, which is what God wants you to do.

God has you on earth for *now*, not for ten years from now. He has a purpose for you ten years from now, too, but you've got to fulfill God's will for you now in order to get there.

Freedom From Fear

If we know what God's plans are for the future, we will be so concerned with what is happening in the ministry today that we won't have any undue concern about the future. We will also better understand our part in God's plan, so we will be free to be fully involved in His work.

The Word of God will set you free! It's the truth that sets you free! Free from concern. Free from worry. Free from anxiety. Free from fear of any kind, including the "great conspiracy" some people picture. They write books — thick books — about it. (I wouldn't bother to read them, if I were you.)

They claim there is a great conspiracy going on in the world. They maintain that Moslems, Communists, Buddhists, Hindus, Capitalists, Socialists, and every other group in existence are involved in this conspiracy to take over the whole world and crush the Church.

Personally, I don't think all these groups could get together and agree on what to have for breakfast tomorrow morning, much less agree on how to take over the whole world! They'd be too busy fighting with each other!

Isaiah even said, "Don't go around saying, 'Conspiracy, conspiracy' " (Isaiah 8:11-13 *New American Standard Bible*). I'm sure that conspiracy *is* occurring in the spirit realm, because the devil conspires against Christians all the time; however, this doesn't mean that everything that happens to you in the natural realm is the result of a demonic conspiracy. Satan is not able to achieve unity among the religious and political groups in the world that are under his sway.

As we saw earlier, this conspiracy theory is one ditch unwary Christians fall into. The opposite ditch is being convinced that the Church is called to straighten out all the problems in the world before Jesus returns.

No, our Commission is to take out of the world a harvest of souls — and we have dominion in this earth to do it. Nothing the devil attempts will prevent us from it. He will surely try, but he won't succeed.

The Seven Spirits

Looking again at verse 4: "...Grace be unto you, and peace, from him which is, and which was, and which is to come; and from the seven Spirits which are before his throne." This verse refers to Jesus Himself.

However, we must understand that there are not seven Holy Spirits. In Isaiah we see that the Holy Spirit is referred to in these different *ways:* He is seen as the spirit of wisdom, understanding, counsel, might, and knowledge (Isaiah 11:2). We already saw Him referred to as the spirit of prophecy in Revelation 19. Sevenfold refers to the *complete* ministry of the Holy Spirit.

Continuing in Revelation 1: "And from Jesus Christ, who is the faithful witness, and the first begotten of the dead, and the prince of the kings of the earth...." (v. 5).

Jesus is the beginning of the Church. He is the first to return from having been separated from God. He became separated because of what He did: He laid down His life for us! He became sin! He didn't *commit* sin; He *became* sin. And He bore for us what would have happened to us had He not become our Substitute.

Washed in the Blood

Now let's look at the rest of verse 5: "Unto him that loved us, and washed us from our sins in his own blood." I've heard people say that you can't find anywhere in the Bible where it says you've got to be washed in the blood. It's right here. Jesus washed us. As one song puts it, He took a black heart that was without love, washed it in red blood, and made it white as snow!

But He didn't stop there. Not only did He put us in right standing with God; "And hath made us kings and priests unto God and his Father; to him be glory and dominion for ever and ever"(v. 6).

Jesus didn't just change our nature; He made us overcomers. He made us worshippers. He made us priests to God — those who would serve Him and do His will in the earth. As kings, He gave us dominion over all the things in the earth.

In the Book of Revelation, we see Jesus' dominion expand to the point where everything comes to perfection. We see it happen the way He said it would.

Verse 7: "Behold, he cometh with clouds; and every eye shall see him, and they also which pierced him: and all kindreds [or families] of the earth [who have not received him] shall wail because of him. Even so, Amen." (In other words, "Come, even so.")

Verse 8: "I am Alpha and Omega, the beginning and the ending, saith the Lord, which is, and which was, and which is to come, the Almighty."

Our God Is Just

God is just. When Jesus returns, there will be those who will rejoice, but there will also be those who will wail because they had every opportunity God could give them to receive the truth, but they rejected these opportunities. It will be just for Jesus to return then, because He will know that all who will choose to accept Him have done so. That's what He is waiting for, as we see below in James 5:7.

"Be patient therefore, brethren, unto the coming of the Lord. Behold, the husbandman [God the Father] waiteth for the precious fruit of the earth, and hath long patience for it, until he receive the early and latter rain."

What is this "precious fruit of the earth"? It is the spirits and souls of men. The word translated as "patience" is actually the Greek word for long-suffering. It means that the Father has long patience with people until He receives the early and the latter rain — that final harvest that His Word foretells.

James goes on in the eighth verse to say, "Be ye also patient; stablish your hearts: for the coming of the Lord draweth nigh."

As you are probably aware, God knows the hearts of men. He will know the exact moment in time when the last person who is going to receive Christ through the work of the Church will have received Him. At that moment, Jesus will return and gather the Church to Himself!

So when Jesus returns and takes His Church home, it will *not* be to snatch us away from the devil just before he devours us; it will be because we have finished the task He gave us to perform!

Jesus told us, "Go and preach the Gospel to every creature." We haven't done that yet. There are entire areas of this world that remain in darkness because they have never heard the Word of God or the name Jesus, and God is waiting for that precious fruit!

Those dark lands are so "ripe" for the Gospel, all you have to do is go plant the seed in them. You don't even need to be eloquent. Just tell the people that God so loved the world that He sent His Son Jesus to save them, heal them, and deliver them, and He's in their midst to help them even then.

You will be amazed at how many hands will go up and how many people will come running to receive Jesus. You don't have to coax them, either; they've been waiting to hear the good news that there is Someone to deliver them. They know they're in a mess. They want out of it, but they don't know how. And they're afraid of demons that hold them in bondage.

In India, despite the fact that masses of people are starving to death all the time, they milk their cows and pour the milk down snake holes as an offering to demon gods. And all this time, their babies are starving to death!

They won't slaughter and eat a cow, because they think one of their relatives may be reincarnated in the animal. When you're starving to death, but you won't partake of food that is right in front of you because of some demonic idea, that's bondage of the worst kind!

However, Jesus' return to take His Bride away will not be a response to escape from what the devil is doing on this earth! The devil will not be any more of a problem to you at the end of time than he is now. In fact, he will be *less* of a problem to you then, because you'll be that much more mature in the Lord!

In Summary

To summarize our study so far, we have seen that the Book of Revelation is an epistle written to the whole Church; it is not a weird book tacked onto the end of the Bible that can only be approached with great fear and trepidation.

I would hate to walk through the streets of heaven, meet the Apostle John, and hear him ask, "Did you enjoy the letter I wrote? Did you profit from reading Revelation?" How embarrassing it would be to have to answer, "No, I never read it." Nor would I want to stand before God and attempt to explain why I didn't read this epistle.

Don't shy away from reading Revelation just because it seemed confusing to you in the past. It will not remain confusing if you approach it the way we will outline. Rely on the Holy Spirit and hold to the conviction that you *need* to study Revelation just like you do any other book of the Bible. In other words, hold the same attitude toward Revelation that you have toward the other books of the Bible.

Also, bear in mind that this epistle is the revelation of Jesus Christ, not the revelation of the anti-Christ, the Great Tribulation, Satan and his angels, or the destruction of the earth, even though all of these things are mentioned in Revelation. The revelation of Jesus Christ includes all of His glory and dominion and shows all of His works being fulfilled in the earth.

In Revelation, you will see things occur all the way from Jesus' first advent to His second advent, and even extend a little beyond that time. But the purpose of Revelation is not to describe our life in eternity; God wants us to focus on what He is doing today on the earth. He shows us just enough to cause us to rejoice and look forward to life in heaven with Him and His Son. (As we read in John 15 and 16 Jesus said that if you're His friend, He will show you "things to come.")

Jesus bore record of the Word of God. The Word of God must always be interpreted in light of itself, nothing else, because the Bible teaches that ". . . no prophecy of the scripture is of any *private interpretation*" (2 Peter 1:20).

As we noted, people have done a great deal of private interpretation of Revelation, even though that was not their intention. They simply failed to realize that Revelation must be interpreted the same way the rest of the Bible is interpreted.

We saw in Revelation 1:3 that special blessings are promised to those who hear and do what is found in the Book of Revelation. I believe that having peace about the turbulent times we're living in is the best part of that special blessing.

This is a momentous hour in which to live. Yes, in the future you will see powerful things happen in the devil's camp, but you will see even more powerful things happen in God's camp!

Knowledge about Jesus and the Father also is to be found in the epistle of Revelation. Second Peter 1:2 says that grace and peace are multiplied to you "through the knowledge of God, and of Jesus our Lord." That's the only way grace and peace come to you.

Chapter 3
The Seven Churches in Asia

John wrote the epistle of Revelation to seven churches. These churches represent the whole Church for the whole age.

Some have wanted to interpret the letter to the first church as covering the first hundred years, the second letter as covering the next two hundred years, and so forth.

The problem with this theory is that you end up with the Laodicean church being backslidden, out of love with God, and powerless! Is that what you are looking forward to: a backslidden, lukewarm Church?

That may be the way the Church has been for a large part of this age, but that's not the way the Church will end up. Paul wrote epistles to churches that were getting that way. And in the second and third chapters of Revelation, the Spirit of God is addressing letters to more of those churches. As a matter of fact, the church at Sardis was already at that point.

Let's imagine that Jesus were writing letters today to churches in these seven modern cities: Fort Worth, Dallas, Oklahoma City, Tulsa, Little Rock, Shreveport, and Kansas City. Reading these letters, we would find Him saying the same things today that He wrote to the seven churches in Asia. The same problems exist today, so the substance of the letters to Asia is just as pertinent to modern Christians as it was to Early Christians.

John: A Companion in Tribulation

But let's go back to Revelation 1:9 for a moment: "I John, who also am your brother, and companion in tribulation, and in the kingdom and patience of Jesus Christ, was in the isle that is called Patmos, for the word of God, and for the testimony of Jesus Christ."

Jesus told His followers, "In the world ye shall have tribulation: but be of good cheer; I have overcome the world" (John 16:33). John knew what Jesus meant, because John suffered a great deal of tribulation during his long life. John lived longer than the other original apostles. The rest of them died martyrs' deaths at different times and in different places.

When John was a bishop of Ephesus, the Roman government became very perturbed with him and his congregation because they wouldn't acknowledge the emperor as a god. They acknowledged him as head of state, but they refused to acknowledge him as the one true, living God. The authorities became so upset with John that they decided to kill him by boiling him in oil.

According to dependable Church tradition, John emerged unscathed, just like Shadrach, Meshach, and Abednego survived the fiery furnace in the Old Testament story in Daniel 3.

Seeing it was impossible to kill John, the authorities decided to exile him to an isolated, rocky island. No doubt they thought, "There's nobody on that island for him to influence. That will take care of him!"

Little could they know that the epistle he would pen on that island would influence all future generations of the very Church they had set out to destroy!

Even though the authorities attempted to kill John on several occasions, he lived out his natural lifespan and finally died at a ripe old age; perhaps in his nineties.

John was a real overcomer! His attitude was, "I'm not going to be defeated, and I won't quit." No matter what happened to him, John got into the Spirit and served God and man.

In the Spirit on the Lord's Day

In Revelation 1:10, John wrote, "I was in the Spirit on the Lord's day, and heard behind me a great voice, as of a trumpet." I believe John means he had been praying in tongues, and he got deeper into the realm of the Spirit than we normally do.

Superspiritual people will try to convince you that they are *always* in the Spirit, but I'm confident that any truly great man of God will tell you he's *not* always in the Spirit. It's a pipe dream to imagine you can live in this world and *always* be in the Spirit. Why? Because you have to spend some time in the natural realm in order to feed and rest your body and do other natural tasks.

John, however, *was* in the Spirit on that Lord's day, and he reports that he heard behind him "a great voice, as of a trumpet." Even though the voice of the Lord is often referred to as being a trumpet voice, it doesn't mean that it *sounds like* a trumpet. It just means that it has the same *effect:* When the Lord speaks like that, you can't miss it!

No one who belongs to Jesus Christ will ever miss the last trumpet. Some people worry, "What if I'm asleep when the Lord comes, the trumpet sounds, and it's time for the Rapture?" Don't worry — you won't miss it! When God wakes you up, you're awake!

The voice behind him told John, "I am Alpha and Omega, the first and the last: and, What thou seest, write in a book, and send it unto the seven churches which are in Asia; unto Ephesus, and unto Smyrna, and unto Pergamos, and unto Thyatira, and unto Sardis, and unto Philadelphia, and unto Laodicea" (v. 11).

These seven towns actually existed in the ancient world; they're not figments of God's imagination that He used to teach some nice little principles.

The Seven Golden Candlesticks

John continues his vision, "And I turned to see the voice that spake with me. And being turned, I saw seven golden candlesticks; And in the midst of the seven candlesticks one like unto the Son of man, clothed with a garment down to the foot, and girt about the paps with a golden girdle" (vv. 12,13).

Gold always symbolizes God's own character. Later on, we will see other examples of the symbol gold. Gold symbolizes divinity, God Himself, and divine things. A candlestick is something that gives light, so we know that this is something God has given that is light-giving. The seven golden candlesticks symbolize the seven churches.

The "one like unto the Son of man" is pictured as being in the middle of the Church. That's where Jesus is, isn't He? Thank God, Jesus is living in us. He is among us. He manifests Himself in our midst.

About His chest is a golden girdle, symbolizing His divine, priestly position as the Son of God and the Son of man.

Verse 14 tells us, "His head and his hairs were white like wool, as white as snow; and his eyes were as a flame of fire." His white head shows us that God has always existed. His eyes like fire symbolize that God is all-knowing, all-wise. His eyes see all things. They see through all facades and all deceit. They see things the way they really are.

God looks upon the heart of man; He doesn't look upon his outward appearance (1 Samuel 16:7). It is useless to try to fool God, even though some people try.

Verses 15 and 16 refer to God's omnipotence in His ability to triumph over all that is resisting Him now. Judgment is symbolized by "feet like unto fine brass," "his voice as the sound of many waters," and "a sharp twoedged sword" going out of His mouth. John responded with reverential awe, and his flesh gave way in the presence of the Exalted Christ.

"I Fell at His Feet"

"And when I saw him," John says in verse 17, "I fell at his feet as dead."

I meet many people who argue, "Well, you can't find any precedent in the Bible for being slain in the Spirit." Accounts of being slain in the Spirit are found throughout the Bible. This is one right here. This is what John is talking about: John was out in the Spirit. He fell.

I have to admit that this has never happened to me. I've stood in prayer lines, and I've cooperated with the Holy Spirit, but I haven't fallen on my face like a dead man. There are times when there isn't any choice in the matter, however. I've seen it happen: People seem to get hit in the knees, and they "buckle." They are just as likely to fall forward; they don't always fall the way you think they're going to. (If you are catching them, you know that from experience.) That's what John is talking about. He just fell — "clunk!" You know he was in the Spirit. He was in the presence of that great manifestation of Jesus appearing to him.

The Keys of Hell and of Death

"And he laid his right hand upon me, saying unto me, Fear not; I am the first and the last: I am he that liveth, and was dead; and, behold, I am alive for evermore, Amen; and have the keys of hell and of death" (vv. 17,18).

What do you think the keys symbolize? Authority and control. Jesus Christ possesses the keys or the control and authority over all things. (The word "hell" here really is Hades, which means all things under the earth.)

As I stated at the beginning of this study, the Book of Revelation thoroughly agrees with the rest of the New Testament. We also see expressed in Philippians 2:9-11 the place of authority Jesus Christ holds in the universe:

> Wherefore God also hath highly exalted him, and given him a name which is above every name: That at the name of Jesus every knee should bow, of things in heaven, and things in earth, and things under the earth; And that every tongue should confess that Jesus Christ is Lord, to the glory of God the Father.

"Things under the earth" are not things that are naturally alive in the human sense. They are *spirit beings* that are no longer alive on the earth, and they're no longer with God; they are separated from Him.

The fact that Jesus holds the keys (or control) over heaven, earth, and things under the earth doesn't mean

He gives the devil his marching orders every morning. It means that Jesus' Name is above all other names — *infinitely* far above them.

Light outshines darkness. Darkness can't prevent the light from shining, even in this dark world, can it? No, and it still doesn't, for Jesus Christ is the Light. We, in turn, are the light of this world, and darkness cannot prevent us from shining.

The Mystery of the Seven Stars

Write the things which thou hast seen, and the things which are, and the things which shall be hereafter; The mystery of the seven stars which thou sawest in my right hand, and the seven golden candlesticks. The seven stars are the angels of the seven churches: and the seven candlesticks which thou sawest are the seven churches.

Revelation 1:19,20

The phrase "things which thou hast seen" is past tense. "Things which are" is present tense. "Things which shall be hereafter" is future tense. So in the succeeding chapters we will find events and happenings which *have happened, are happening,* and *will happen.* (We realize that some events referred to have changed their tense by now, but all three tenses are still used accurately and have been since John received this Revelation.)

The "stars" represent angels or messengers. In some cases, that word is translated "human messengers." I believe this is the case here. The Spirit of God is addressing the churches, not the angelic host. He's writing to us, isn't He? Therefore, I conclude He is writing this epistle to those who are in authority over these churches — the messengers of God in these seven churches.

As we read, the seven candlesticks symbolize the seven churches. Remember, we saw that the candlesticks were golden, symbolizing divinity: God Himself and the light. They bear light. Of course, the Church bears light. We are the light of the world.

The Church of the Lord Jesus Christ is becoming a Bride without spot, wrinkle, or blemish — a glorious Church that Jesus will receive to Himself after the Body has completed the work He gave it to do.

Summary of Chapters Two and Three

The second and third chapters of Revelation are seven letters (or epistles) to seven churches. In them, we see the Head of the Church, the Lord Jesus Christ, ministering to the whole Church, His Body, for the whole Age of Grace.

These letters summarize His commendations for, warnings to, and promises to overcomers. All of them are entirely consistent with other New Testament writings, and they are as applicable to us today as they were when the Apostle John wrote them under the unction of the Holy Spirit and sent them to the seven churches.

These seven short epistles continue the emphasis on the Church of Jesus Christ and its mission in this world. They are full of blessings, grace, and revelations; and, Lord willing, I plan to make them the subject of a separate book.

I believe that the seven letters point the way to what is found in chapters four through seven — the victorious conclusion to the Age of Grace!

Chapter 4
The Throne of God

A proper understanding of chapters four and five is necessary to understand chapter six.

What we have seen so far in our study is Jesus revealing Himself to John and telling him what He wanted done. And as Jesus revealed Himself as the glorified Christ, He communicated grace and peace to the churches. Next, He wrote to the seven churches that represent the whole Church for the whole age.

Now, in chapters four and five, John will be caught away into heaven and will see things that are the result of the Church Age.

The Piercing Voice of God

Chapter four opens with the piercing voice of God Himself: "After this I looked, and, behold, a door was opened in heaven: and the first voice which I heard was as it were of a trumpet talking with me; which said, Come up hither, and I will shew thee things which must be hereafter."

So John is going to be caught away into heaven by the agency of the Holy Spirit, and there he will see things *as they have been, as they are,* and *as they will be.*

Verses two and three continue, "And immediately I was in the spirit: and, behold, a throne was set in heaven, and one sat on the throne. And he that sat was to look upon like a jasper and a sardine stone: and there was a rainbow round about the throne, in sight like unto an emerald."

John, in describing brilliant, many-faceted stones, doesn't tell us what God looks like, but he does paint a vivid picture of the effect of God's presence: a dazzling rainbow of light, reflected many different ways. This description of God's presence is as close as the Bible comes to describing what God looks like.

"And round about the throne were four and twenty seats: and upon the seats I saw four and twenty elders sitting, clothed in white raiment; and they had on their heads crowns of gold" (v. 4).

These elders represent the redeemed from *all* ages, not just the Church Age. For example, we see in Ephesians 4:8 that after Jesus rose from the dead, He "led captivity captive," ascended, and gave gifts to men. One application of this verse is that Jesus removed all the souls who were in paradise (see Luke 16), awaiting His coming so they could be born again. In other words, when Jesus was raised from the dead, they were, too.

Caught Up Into Paradise

Jesus took these spirits of "just men made perfect" (before Calvary) to heaven with Him. By this action, He transferred "paradise" from a place that had been beneath the earth up into heaven itself.

Paul states in Second Corinthians 12 that he was caught *up* into paradise in a vision. So paradise wasn't beneath the earth anymore, for Paul was caught *up* into heaven. Paradise is now in the presence of God, in heaven. Furthermore, we see in Second Corinthians

5:8 and other verses that if you are absent from your body, you are present with the Lord!

The four and twenty elders represent all the redeemed who are in the presence of God, whether from this current age or an earlier age. They have run their race; they have finished their course.

"And out of the throne proceeded lightnings and thunderings and voices: and there were seven lamps of fire burning before the throne, which are the seven Spirits of God" (v. 5).

Believe me, you can go overboard in studying numerology, but numbers do have some significance. God does use numbers to illustrate certain principles. For example, the number seven represents fulfillment or completion.

Redemption Fulfilled!

In this chapter we see the complete picture of God Himself and those who are redeemed in His presence: *The fulfillment of the work of Redemption.* It is a picture of Jesus Christ's work being fulfilled before it happens — for *one aspect of the redemptive work of Jesus is still being fulfilled today in the earth.* Of course, Jesus finished the work of Redemption on the cross, but we are to finish telling the world about it — proclaiming the Good News — as Luke suggests in Acts 1:1.

Here in the fourth and fifth chapters of Revelation, we see the work of Redemption completed and the results of it. Then, in chapter six, we will see an account of *how* it was and will be done. We will see what is to happen in the Age of Grace, *prophesied before it happens!*

Remember, we are seeing these events from God's perspective. All things are "now" with Him, for He is outside the limits of time; He exists in eternity.

In Revelation 4:5, we read about lightnings, thunderings, and voices proceeding out of God's throne. That is God communicating with the Church. He communicates *continually.* And there were seven lamps of fire burning before the throne — the seven Spirits of God, or the fullness of the Holy Spirit.

Verse 6: "And before the throne there was a sea of glass like unto crystal...." It is interesting to note how the word "sea" is used throughout Revelation, for it represents a great mass. Again, this sea of glass represents the great mass of the redeemed. They are likened unto clear crystal, because they have been purified; they reflect the light.

The Four Living Creatures

The verse continues, "...and in the midst of the throne, and round about the throne, were four beasts full of eyes before and behind." There are many references to "beasts" in Revelation. Most translations use the term "living creatures" in this verse. The Greek word here is *zoon,* which comes from *zoe,* which means life. Angelic beings is what they really are; a special category of angel.

Whenever we encounter these four living creatures, they are always seen with the twenty-four elders. They are meant to be viewed *together,* not separately. The meaning of their eyes being "before and behind" is that they possess great wisdom and knowledge.

"And the first beast was like a *lion,* and the second beast like a *calf,* and the third beast had a face as a *man,* and the fourth beast was like a *flying eagle*" (v. 7). The Holy Spirit is making an analogy here, comparing the beasts to other things.

"And the four beasts had each of them six wings about him; and they were full of eyes within: and they rest not day and night, saying, Holy, holy, holy, Lord God Almighty, which was, and is, and is to come" (v. 8). They are in the presence of God, and they are magnifying Him day and night.

"And when those beasts give glory and honour and thanks to him that sat on the throne, who liveth for ever and ever, The four and twenty elders fall down before him that sat on the throne, and worship him that liveth for ever and ever, and cast their crowns before the throne, saying, Thou art worthy, O Lord, to receive glory and honour and power: for thou hast created all things, and for thy pleasure they are and were created" (vv. 9-11).

Now let's look back at verse seven and study those four living creatures. The first is described as being like a lion, "the king of the beasts." The lion has a place above the other animals: he is a king, a conqueror. So this living creature represents Jesus as being the lion of the Tribe of Judah. In that sense, Jesus conquered all things.

Important to God

This angelic being represents something that is of paramount importance in the very presence of God. We are not saying that the living creatures did the works implied, for they did not. They represent the works that are of primary importance in the sight of God; thus, the first living creature is *like* a lion.

The second living creature, the calf, represents a servant — and even more — because the calf when grown is an ox, a beast of burden.

Jesus, who is the mighty Conqueror, left glory and His divine attributes as the King of kings to become a man. And when He became human, He became the Servant of mankind. He said, ". . .the Son of man came not to be ministered unto, but to minister. . ." (Matthew 20:28). He became the Servant of all, starting with His own disciples.

The calf represents all that and more. The calf also represents Jesus' sacrifice. He was sacrificed for man under the Old Covenant. So He who is the King of kings and the mighty Conqueror became the Servant and the Sacrifice for mankind.

The third living creature had a face like a man. It was man who needed to be redeemed; and it was as man that Jesus, the second member of the Godhead, did the work of Redemption. He became a man — wholly, fully human — and did that work. He did it to redeem the man who had blundered and fallen so that fallen man could be like the fourth creature — an eagle!

The fourth creature is like an eagle. An eagle extends his wings and floats effortlessly toward heaven on the updrafts. He lives in lofty places. Hallelujah, he's an overcomer!

The King Becomes a Servant

Now you can see the complete picture: The King of kings, the mighty Conqueror, left glory and became the Servant of man and the Sacrifice for man. Why? So that man, who had sinned and fallen from the presence of God, could be restored and become an overcomer!

Redemption, the theme of this whole passage, is of paramount importance to God. Everything else in His presence is of less importance. We see the work of Redemption that God Himself did in the Son signified by the four supernatural, angelic beings.

And whenever these creatures give glory, honor, and thanks to the Father, the four and twenty elders, representing all the redeemed, fall on their faces before the throne and worship Him, casting their crowns before Him, saying, "Thou art worthy, O Lord, to receive glory and honour and power. . . ."

"Isn't Jesus already glorified?" you may ask. Yes, He is, and John was seeing this. But Jesus is going to receive *more* glory as His Body, the Church, performs His will. This glorifies Him: ". . . for thou hast created all things, and for thy pleasure they are and were created."

As we saw in James 5:7, the Lord has long patience for the precious fruit of the earth. As He waits and shows us His long-suffering, we see Him glorified in that, because He will receive it! God did not devise a plan that does not work; He has a plan that does work. He *will* have the precious fruit of the earth that He has had long patience for.

Chapter 5
The Book With Seven Seals

A nd I saw in the right hand of him that sat on the throne a book written within and on the backside, sealed with seven seals" (Revelation 5:1). This "book" is actually a scroll, written on both sides, rolled up, and sealed at various points.

In chapters five and six we will see the result of the work the Church does.

> And I saw a strong angel proclaiming with a loud voice, Who is worthy to open the book, and to loose the seals thereof?
>
> And no man in heaven, nor in earth, neither under the earth, was able to open the book, neither to look thereon.
>
> And I wept much, because no man was found worthy to open and to read the book, neither to look thereon.
>
> And one of the elders saith unto me, Weep not: behold, the Lion of the tribe of Juda, the Root of David, hath prevailed to open the book, and to loose the seven seals thereof.
>
> And I beheld, and, lo, in the midst of the throne and of the four beasts, and in the midst of the elders, stood a Lamb as it had been slain, having seven horns and seven eyes, which are the seven Spirits of God sent forth into all the earth.
>
> Revelation 5:2-6

The Authority of the Lamb

Here, Jesus is pictured not as the King of kings, and not as One taking authority to rule and reign upon the earth. Instead, He is pictured as the Redeemer, the Lamb of God. The seven horns represent perfect authority, and the seven eyes represent the all-knowing seven Spirits of God. Notice that the Redeemer is seen "in the midst of the throne."

> **And he came and took the book out of the right hand of him that sat upon the throne.**
>
> **And when he had taken the book, the four beasts and four and twenty elders fell down before the Lamb, having every one of them harps, and golden vials full of odours, which are the prayers of saints.**
>
> **Revelation 5:7,8**

The prayers of the saints are depicted as vials full of sweet-smelling odors! Those prayers we prayed in the past are recorded in heaven! They have had their effect, and they are *still* having their effect.

Even though Christians may have prayed for some things that never came to pass during their lifetime, that doesn't mean that their prayers won't be answered. Those vials are stored in heaven. The prayers were effectual — and they will continue to be effectual.

Redeemed Out of Every Nation

> **And they sung a new song, saying, Thou art worthy to take the book, and to open the seals thereof: for thou wast slain, and hast redeemed us to God by thy blood out of every kindred, and tongue, and people, and nation.**
>
> **Revelation 5:9**

"Every kindred" means every family group; "every tongue" means every language group; "every people," every racial group; and "every nation," every national group. No matter how you divide it, people will be redeemed out of every group on the face of the earth.

The next verse continues, "And hast made us unto our God kings and priests: and we shall reign on the earth" (v. 10).

Let's go back for a moment and re-examine the scroll that was described at the beginning of chapter five. If the contents of this scroll merely show us what will come after the Church finishes its work, as some people maintain, then the scroll is nothing more than a deed to the earth that Jesus will open before beginning His reign on earth. In that case, we will truly see great tribulation from now to the end of the age.

What the Scroll Contains

I think that the scroll does contain the deed to the earth, but much more. I believe it also contains what Jesus did as the Redeemer of mankind, *because only Jesus can open the scroll!* What work is reserved to Jesus alone? The work of Redemption! He's the Redeemer. No other could do that work; He's the only One.

If the scroll merely contained prophecies, Daniel, Paul, Peter, and others could open it, because God inspired many men by the Holy Spirit to write about the future.

So I do not see an emphasis here on simply telling us what is to happen in the future. I see the emphasis as being the work that Jesus did as the Redeemer. A little further on, in verse six, we see the phrase, "in the midst of the elders, stood a Lamb...."

What we are going to see, then, is the work Jesus *did* as the Lamb of God — the Redeemer — not the work He *will do* in the future as the King of kings. (We'll see that later on in the Book of Revelation.)

The Church Will Succeed!

In verses seven through nine, the Holy Spirit shows us all the elements that are characteristic of this age: what Jesus set out to do, and what remains to be done. I'm glad the Holy Spirit showed this to us, because from these few verses, *you can know with perfect assurance that the Church is going to succeed!* You don't have to wonder about it.

Of course, if you simply studied Church history, you would conclude that we will never get this job done! The Church has never yet finished a job that God gave it to do!

The first century church did an excellent job, but they only touched a small part of the world, whereas Jesus told us to go into *all* the world. The Church has never completed this task.

At the time of this writing, more than half the world remains in total darkness, having never heard the Gospel. You may find that difficult to believe, after all the people who have been sent out as missionaries, yet it is a fact. More than half of the world's population has never heard the Gospel.

Did you know that half the world's population lives in two nations — India and China? There are more than a billion persons in China and nearly a billion in India at the present time — and the majority of them have never heard the Good News.

Do you think God is just going to bypass them? No, He's not! He's raising up people to go into those dark places to preach the Gospel to every creature, just like Jesus said.

If the Church does not succeed in preaching the Gospel to every creature, God's Word would return to Him void, and it cannot.

That's what I like about the Book of Revelation: You see the Church *succeeding;* you see the Church *overcoming;* you see the Church *finishing* the work it has been given to do on earth. So you don't have to wonder whether we're going to make it or not, despite history and despite circumstances.

Look instead to the Word of God. You will see your part of the job. Do it with all of your might. Don't worry about the rest of the Church. God knows what He is doing. He has a plan that works, and every believer is a part of that plan.

Thank God, He has given us the personal, individual vision to see what our part is. It's good for us to see the whole plan of Revelation and know that God has everything under control. The Body of Christ *will* succeed in fulfilling the Great Commission! There is no doubt about it.

Innumerable Angels Assist Us

In verse 11, John heard the voice of "many angels round about the throne and the beasts and the elders: and the number of them was ten thousand times ten thousand, and thousands of thousands." That's hundreds of millions of angels, but I don't think it's supposed to be taken as a limit; instead, it's an expression for a countless multitude.

In Hebrews 12:22, it says there is an innumerable company of angels — more than we could count, or more than enough to help us do the work Jesus has given us to do. And believe me, He gave the angels to us for help, and He means for them to help us.

Verse 12 continues, "Saying with a loud voice, Worthy is the Lamb that was slain to receive power, and riches, and wisdom, and strength, and honour, and glory, and blessing."

This is what the Lord Jesus Christ receives from the obedient Body that will fulfill His will on this earth. When God gathers the precious fruit of the earth, Jesus will receive all of these things to Himself.

Chapter five concludes with these words:

> And every creature which is in heaven, and on the earth, and under the earth, and such as are in the sea, and all that are in them, heard I saying, Blessing, and honour, and glory, and power, be unto him that sitteth upon the throne, and unto the Lamb for ever and ever.
>
> And the four beasts said, Amen. And the four and twenty elders fell down and worshipped him that liveth for ever and ever.
>
> **Revelation 5:13,14**

In chapter six we will see the Lamb of God opening those seals — again, not as the King of kings to rule over the earth — *but as the Lamb of God to redeem it.* And as we see what He does and what happens when He opens those seven seals, the history of our age will be unrolled before our eyes.

Chapter 6
The Scrolls Are Opened

Remember, John is viewing his revelation from God's perspective, and God sees everything as *now*. To God, events aren't "yesterday," "today," or "tomorrow"; they are *now*. In other words, everything to God is in the present tense! So as we look at the events in chapters four, five, and six of the Book of Revelation, we must bear in mind that God is seeing them as happening *now*.

From our human perspective, most of what John saw is in the future, starting from the time that he received the vision. However, some of the revelation had already occurred, and some of it was occurring at the time of John's vision. That's why Revelation must be studied both from man's point of view and from God's point of view.

In the fourth chapter, we saw that there was a great emphasis on Redemption around the throne of God. The four living creatures symbolize the work of Redemption. The great sea of glass represents the great mass of the redeemed who will be in heaven. *John is looking then into the future, but he is seeing it as a present fact.*

And bear in mind, as we mentioned earlier, that the Book of Revelation is *not* written in chronological order. People put too much weight on the chronology and not enough on the content. You can miss a great deal by trying to make it all come out in chronological order.

The Lamb Reveals the Church Age

What we are about to see in chapter six is not just what will happen in the Great Tribulation. Instead, the chapter covers the whole Age of Grace (or Church Age) we are presently living in, from the time that Jesus did the work of Redemption until now — and even beyond.

The chapter opens with the words, "And I saw when the Lamb opened one of the seals, and I heard, as it were the noise of thunder, one of the four beasts saying, Come and see."

It is not the King of kings or the Lord of lords who is opening the scroll; it is the Lamb. We know it's Jesus, but He is doing it as the Redeemer of mankind, not as the King or the Judge of those who rejected the truth.

Jesus is the only One who can open the seal, and He did. The four living creatures are involved in this, and again they symbolize the work of Redemption.

The Mystery of the White Horse

"And I saw, and behold, a white horse: and he that sat on him had a bow; and a crown was given unto him: and he went forth conquering, and to conquer" (v. 2).

There are some fine, sincere Christians who will tell you that the person riding the white horse represents the anti-Christ, so let's explore what the color white and the horse symbolize.

If you really want to understand the Book of Revelation, you will need to apply yourself and study, and you will need a good concordance to help you discover what certain things symbolize throughout the Bible.

If you'll look up all the scripture references the concordance shows for a certain word, you will see how that word is used throughout the Bible, and what it symbolizes when it is used symbolically.

First, the Color White

We'll take the time at this point to do a simple study, using the color white. It isn't difficult to do such a study; it just takes some work. You can't skim the surface and expect the whole meaning of Revelation to fall into place! But when you devote some time to study this book, God will show you many things.

First of all, throughout the Bible, *white symbolizes the characteristics of God*, including holiness, purity, peace, and righteousness.

For example, turn to Isaiah 1:18, where God says, "Come now, and let us reason together, saith the Lord: though your sins be as scarlet, they shall be as white as snow; though they be red like crimson, they shall be as wool." So in this verse, white symbolizes *cleansing,* or the work of regeneration.

Daniel 11:35 is referring to the time of the Great Tribulation, according to its context: "And some of them of [natural or perhaps religious] understanding shall fall, to try them, and to purge, and to make them white, even to the time of the end: because it is yet for a time appointed." Here, white stands for *righteousness.*

The color white has a slightly different meaning in Matthew 17:1,2. "And after six days Jesus taketh Peter, James, and John his brother, and bringeth them up into an high mountain apart, And was transfigured before them: and his face did shine as the sun, and his raiment was white as the light." Jesus' robe glistened. So white symbolizes *light*, too. God is light!

Now let's look at another example in Matthew 28. When Mary Magdalene and Mary went to the sepulchre to attend to the body of Jesus, "behold, there was a great earthquake: for the angel of the Lord descended from heaven, and came and rolled back the stone from the door, and sat upon it. His countenance was like lightning, and his raiment white as snow" (vv. 2,3). Here, *a godly being* is symbolized as such by white raiment.

Another case is seen in the angels who spoke to the disciples as Jesus ascended from the Mount of Olives: "And while they [the disciples] looked stedfastly toward heaven as he went up, behold, two men stood by them in white apparel. . ." (Acts 1:10). We know the two men were angels of God because of their apparel.

We can also see in Revelation 3:4 where Jesus said, "Thou hast a few names even in Sardis which have not defiled their garments; and they shall walk with me in white: for they are worthy. . . ." They shall walk "in white": in holiness, in purity, in peace.

White Never Symbolizes Evil

This is just a quick look at a few scriptures showing what white symbolizes. As you delve into the scriptures for yourself, you will not find any verses where white symbolizes the devil or any of his works. So why anyone would suddenly decide when he gets to chapter six that the color symbolizes the anti-Christ, I can't imagine.

Do you think that God is going to use one color to symbolize Himself throughout scripture and then turn around and use the same symbol to depict the devil? I don't believe so. I don't think God is short of symbols. And I believe He can think just as well as we can. So I don't think it's sensible to say at this point that white symbolizes the anti-Christ, despite what others teach on the matter.

Furthermore, many books have been written about the four horses of the apocalypse that make it sound like all of chapter six takes place in the Great Tribulation, all of it involves judgment, and all hell breaks loose on the earth. I think you'll miss the main point if you view the chapter this way!

But let's look at Psalm 45 before we go any further.

> **My heart is inditing a good matter: I speak of the things which I have made touching the king: my tongue is the pen of a ready writer.**
>
> **Thou art fairer than the children of men: grace is poured into thy lips: therefore God hath blessed thee for ever.**
>
> **Gird thy sword upon thy thigh, O most mighty, with thy glory and thy majesty.**
>
> **And in thy majesty ride prosperously because of truth and meekness and righteousness; and thy right hand shall teach thee terrible things.**
>
> **Thine arrows are sharp in the heart of the king's enemies; whereby the people fall under thee.**
>
> **Thy throne, O God, is for ever and ever: the sceptre of thy kingdom is a right sceptre.**
>
> **Thou lovest righteousness, and hatest wickedness: therefore God, thy God, hath anointed thee with the oil of gladness above thy fellows.**
>
> **Psalm 45:1-7**

Is there any doubt in your mind about the subject of David's prophecy? This is the work that Jesus will do! He is shown going forth as a man of war, to conquer. He is shown going forth to achieve and acquire something: "In thy majesty ride prosperously because of truth and meekness and righteousness," it says, "and thy right hand shall teach thee terrible things" (v. 4).

The Horse in Symbolism

Now we must learn what the *horse* symbolizes. Let's start with the story in Second Kings 6, where the king of Syria sent horses and chariots after the prophet Elisha.

Elisha's servant saw them and was terrified. Elisha reassured him with the words, "Fear not: for they that be with us are more than they that be with them" (v. 16). Then the prophet said, "Lord, I pray thee, open his eyes, that he may see.

"And the Lord opened the eyes of the young man; and he saw: and, behold, the mountain was full of *horses* and chariots of fire round about Elisha" (v. 17).

There is no symbolic meaning to the army of *natural* horses and chariots the king sent after the prophet. However, the *supernatural* horses and chariots of fire around Elisha symbolize *spiritual warfare*; in this case, angelic beings sent to fight on the prophet's behalf.

Another reference to horses is found in Exodus 15:1. "Then sang Moses and the children of Israel, . . . I will sing unto the Lord, for he hath triumphed gloriously: the horse and his rider hath he thrown into the sea."

They were singing about the fact that Pharaoh and his army, with their horses and chariots, had been drowned. Later in this chapter, Moses' sister, Miriam, said, "Sing ye to the Lord, for he hath triumphed gloriously; the horse and his rider hath he thrown into the sea" (v. 21).

There is a natural meaning in these passages, but they also contain a spiritual message for us today. When we sing them as a chorus, are we celebrating the Jews' victory over Pharaoh, or are we celebrating what Jesus did? Jesus unseated powers and principalities in the spirit realm, so there is a symbolic use of the "horse and rider" that Jesus "threw into the sea," or unseated and conquered.

Jesus Wages Spiritual Warfare for Us

Another passage that speaks prophetically about Jesus' waging spiritual warfare is found in Habakkuk 3.

> Was the Lord displeased against the rivers? was thine anger against the rivers? was thy wrath against the sea, that thou didst ride upon thine horses and thy chariots of salvation?
>
> Thy bow was made quite naked, according to the oaths of the tribes, even thy word. Selah. Thou didst cleave the earth with rivers.
>
> The mountains saw thee, and they trembled: the overflowing of the water passed by: the deep uttered his voice, and lifted up his hands on high.
>
> The sun and moon stood still in their habitation: at the light of thine arrows they went, and at the shining of thy glittering spear.
>
> Thou didst march through the land in indignation, thou didst thresh the heathen in anger.
>
> Thou wentest forth for the salvation of thy people, even for salvation with thine anointed; thou woundest the head out of the house of the wicked....
>
> Habakkuk 3:8-13

Jesus was manifested to do what? Destroy the works of the devil! Break them up. Render them ineffective. Did He do it? Yes, He did! In the above passage, Habakkuk is prophesying about Jesus' waging warfare, and he's also prophesying about God riding on horses and chariots of salvation. His topic is spiritual warfare.

Returning to Revelation 6:2, we see Jesus seated upon what? A white horse. Although it doesn't say He is the rider of the white horse, we understand that He is, because of the symbolic nature of white horses. When *a horse* is mentioned by itself, it doesn't symbolize godly warfare; however, when it is described as *a white horse*, that symbolizes godly warfare.

Again, Revelation 6:2 reads, "And I saw, and behold a white horse: and he that sat on him had a bow; and a crown was given unto him: and he went forth conquering, and to conquer." Notice Jesus goes forth alone — no one is with Him. He doesn't have any help. He doesn't have any army.

He has a bow, but He doesn't have any arrows for His bow as yet. Why? Because He is the first. He is the beginning. He is the firstborn from the dead. He is the first among many brethren, it says in Romans 8:29. It is He who went and conquered the enemy. It is He who conquered death. And it is He who set us all free so we could follow Him!

A Later Appearance on Horseback

It is helpful at this point to turn to Revelation 19 to see another appearance of Jesus that occurs later in time.

> Let us be glad and rejoice, and give honour to him: for the marriage of the Lamb is come, and his wife hath made herself ready.
>
> And to her was granted that she should be arrayed in fine linen, clean and white: for the fine linen is the righteousness of saints.

And he saith unto me, Write, Blessed are they which are called unto the marriage supper of the Lamb. And he saith unto me, These are the true sayings of God.

And I fell at his feet to worship him. And he said unto me, See thou do it not: I am thy fellowservant, and of thy brethren that have the testimony of Jesus: worship God: for the testimony of Jesus is the spirit of prophecy.

And I saw heaven opened, and behold *a white horse; and he that sat upon him was called Faithful and True, and in righteousness he doth judge and make war.*

His eyes were as a flame of fire, and on his head were many crowns; and he had a name written, that no man knew, but he himself.

And he was clothed with a vesture dipped in blood: and *his name is called The Word of God.*

And *the armies which were in heaven followed him upon white horses,* clothed in fine linen, white and clean.

And out of his mouth goeth a sharp sword, that with it he should smite the nations: and he shall rule them with a rod of iron: and he treadeth the winepress of the fierceness and wrath of Almighty God.

And he hath on his vesture and on his thigh a name written, KING OF KINGS, AND LORD OF LORDS.

Revelation 19:7-16

Here we see Jesus coming to reign upon the earth. The armies that are in heaven come with Him. Notice their position. They're not here on the earth, about to meet Jesus in the clouds. At this point, they have *already* done that. Now they're *with Him in heaven,* and they're coming with Him, to reign with Him upon the earth.

And they're all riding upon white horses. Why? *Because they're all waging spiritual warfare!*

So Jesus is not alone anymore; He's got a whole army with Him. (He did His work alone in Revelation 6 so He could have this army now.)

If you believe the horseman of chapter six is the anti-Christ, you will miss a great deal of what the rest of the chapter unfolds. In it, I believe God is telling us what will happen in the future. We will see some good Church history later in the chapter. (But because we are living at the *end* of the Church Age, those verses will be history to us, because they have already been fulfilled.)

We also will see something that many people wonder about at times because of the disappointing history of the Church. Although it is important to study past Church history, you need to go beyond it and learn the victorious future God has planned for it. If you dwell on the history of the Church, all you will see are small degrees of success and a great deal of failure!

More than half the world — almost 3 billion people — have never heard the Gospel! Never. Not once. Just a few years ago, 95 percent of the ministers in the world were preaching to five percent of the world's population. I don't think that is pleasing to God. Thank God for His patience. He knows all of us must be prepared before that work can be finished, but He said He would do a quick work at the end of this dispensation, once His people are ready to do His will.

God's New Bow: The Believers

Returning once again to chapter six, let us look at the first verse: "And I saw when the Lamb opened one of the seals, and I heard, as it were the noise of thunder, one of the four beasts saying, Come and see. And I saw, and behold a white horse: and he that sat on him had a bow..." (vv. 1,2).

Back in Habakkuk 3:9 we saw the statement, "Thy bow was made quite naked, according to the oaths of the tribes, even thy word. Selah...."

That bow is another symbol of spiritual warfare, of course. The prophet is referring to the tribes of Israel, for there was a day when Israel chose idolatry over serving God — and they were judged and went into captivity for it.

That made God's bow naked, for precious few remained who chose to believe in Him. It made His means of waging warfare in the earth ineffectual: His bow was made quite naked, "according to the oaths of the tribes," or their disobedience.

However, God was not defeated. He knew those things would happen. Thank God, there has always been a believing remnant in this earth who have believed God, and God has worked through these people who believe His Word.

Reading on in Habakkuk 3, we see that the Lord did something about the naked bow. It says in the eleventh verse, "The sun and moon stood still in their habitation: at the light of thine arrows they went, and at the shining of thy glittering spear." This shows that God's arrows will be fired again; His bow will once again be functional.

Verses 12 and 13: "Thou didst march through the land in indignation, thou didst thresh the heathen in anger. Thou wentest forth for the salvation of thy people, even for salvation with thine anointed; *thou woundest the head out of the house of the wicked...*"

This prophecy is about Jesus! He destroyed — broke up — the works of the enemy!

Remember, in Revelation 6:2 it says that the rider on the horse had a bow — but it doesn't say anything about arrows yet.

Chapter 7
Gentiles in the Age of Grace

Israel was God's battle bow under the Old Covenant, and the individual Israelites were His arrows. It was through them that He would wage spiritual warfare on the earth. Eventually He reclaimed the earth and redeemed its inhabitants through Jesus Christ's first coming as the Messiah.

In Psalm 18:13,14 we read, "The Lord also thundered in the heavens, and the Highest gave his voice; hail stones and coals of fire. Yea, he sent out his arrows, and scattered them; and he shot out lightnings, and discomfited them." Now, to shoot arrows, what do you have to have? A bow! So we see God is using something to launch spiritual warfare here.

Look at Psalm 21:11-13: "For they intended evil against thee: they imagined a mischievous device, which they are not able to perform. Therefore shalt thou make them turn their back, when thou shalt make ready thine arrows upon thy strings against the face of them. Be thou exalted, Lord, in thine own strength: so will we sing and praise thy power."

Again, if you're going to launch any arrows, you must have a bow. Israel was the battle bow, but we saw in Habakkuk that bow was made naked. And there were no arrows to fire. In other words, through their disobedience, the children of Israel limited God, didn't they? They limited the Holy One of Israel! (Psalm 78:41.) Israel was then cut off as the battle bow.

Look now at Zechariah 9:9,10: "Rejoice greatly, O daughter of Zion; shout, O daughter of Jerusalem: behold, thy King cometh unto thee: he is just, and having salvation; lowly, and riding upon an ass, and upon a colt the foal of an ass. And I will cut off the chariot from Ephraim, and the horse from Jerusalem, and *the battle bow shall be cut off....*" That's what happened, isn't it?

Israel was God's covenant people, but they broke His covenant over and over again. When Jesus came, they rejected Him, for the most part. However, there *was* a remnant of Jews who accepted Jesus as the Messiah, and Paul mentions this "remnant according to the election of grace" in Romans 11:5.

Because Israel as a whole rejected and crucified His Son, God broke them off as the battle bow. The Old Covenant was finished. Who do you suppose is the battle bow today? *The Church!*

And who are God's arrows today? *You are* — Spirit-filled men and women who speak the Word of God from a believing heart. People who heal, deliver, and lead others into salvation. People who build up the waste places. Today you're the arrows, and the Church is the battle bow.

But the prophet Zechariah couldn't see that; he prophesies further. He didn't know there was going to be an Age of Grace. Yes, some of the Old Testament prophets prophesied about the Age of Grace, but not one of them understood it.

Even some of Jesus' disciples didn't understand when He told them about it. They kept looking to Him to rule and reign on the earth. Even in the first chapter of Acts, when Jesus was about to ascend into heaven, they were still asking Him, "Well, will You now reign over Israel?" "No, not yet," He answered. They didn't understand that there was going to be an age when God would visit all the Gentiles and take out of them a people for His Name.

The Jews' Future Role in History

So we read that the prophet Zechariah saw that the chariot was cut off from Ephraim and the horse from Jerusalem. (They stand for both the northern and southern kingdoms.) The passage continues:

> ...and he shall speak peace unto the heathen: and his dominion shall be from sea even to sea, and from the river even to the ends of the earth [the whole earth]
>
> As for thee also, by the blood of thy covenant I have sent forth thy prisoners out of the pit wherein is no water.
>
> Turn you to the strong hold, ye prisoners of hope: even to day do I declare that I will render double unto thee;
>
> When I have bent Judah for me, filled the bow with Ephraim, and raised up thy sons, O Zion, against thy sons, O Greece, and made thee as the sword of a mighty man.
>
> And the Lord shall be seen over them, and his arrow shall go forth as the lightning: and the Lord God shall blow the trumpet, and shall go with whirlwinds of the south.
>
> The Lord of hosts shall defend them; and they shall devour, and subdue with sling stones; and they shall drink, and make a noise as through wine; and they shall be filled like bowls, and as the corners of the altar.

> And the Lord their God shall save them in that
> day as the flock of his people: for they shall be as the
> stones of a crown, lifted up as an ensign upon his
> land.
>
> For how great is his goodness, and how great is
> his beauty! corn shall make the young men cheerful,
> and new wine the maids.
>
> **Zechariah 9:10-17**

So you see, there's a day coming when Israel will
enter into the New Covenant. There's a day coming
when God will once again use them as His battle bow.
There's a day coming when they will once again be the
arrows you are today.

Actually, the Jews will be in the same covenant —
the New Covenant — we Gentiles are in today. That's
what Zechariah is prophesying to them. Notice he
didn't say a word about the Church or the Church Age,
because he's prophesying to the Jews about their future
and what their role will be in it.

So Jesus is seen in Revelation 6:2 as sitting on a
white horse with a bow, "and he went forth conquering,
and to conquer." However, He is represented as
conquering alone; He has no arrows yet. Through the
cross and His Resurrection, all the power of the enemy
is rendered ineffectual. Dominion is then restored to
believers, making them like Jesus. For Jesus was
manifested to destroy, break up, and render ineffectual
the works of the enemy.

Going back to Revelation 1:4-6, John says that grace
and peace are coming to the Church "from Jesus Christ,
who is the faithful witness, and the first begotten of
the dead [that's how He destroyed the works of the
devil], and the prince of the kings of the earth [for He
is the King of kings and the Lord of lords].

"Unto him that loved us, and washed us from our sins in his own blood, And hath made us kings and priests unto God and his Father; to him be glory and dominion for ever and ever. Amen." This is a forecast of what we will see later, in more detail, in chapter six.

The Work of Redemption

The work of Redemption that Jesus did is described in more detail in Colossians 1:

> And he is the head of the body, the church: who is the beginning, the firstborn from the dead; that in all things he might have the preeminence.
>
> For it pleased the Father that in him should all fulness dwell;
>
> And, having made peace through the blood of his cross, by him to reconcile all things unto himself; by him, I say, whether they be things in earth, or things in heaven.
>
> And you, that were sometime alienated and enemies in your mind by wicked works, yet now hath he reconciled.
>
> In the body of his flesh through death, to present you holy and unblameable and unreproveable in his sight:
>
> If ye continue in the faith grounded and settled, and be not moved away from the hope of the gospel....
>
> **Colossians 1:18-23**

Jesus did the work of Redemption. He did reconcile man to God. What does it mean to "reconcile"? It means to remove the differences that existed between two individuals. Even some people who are saved don't know it yet, but it's still true: Jesus removed the differences between God and man. He reconciled us!

When I was a young officer in the Air Force, we had to inventory the commissary and the PX each month by counting everything on the shelves or in the packing cases. A man right behind us would also count everything. When we got done, we compared lists, and if they weren't alike, they had to be reconciled. The difference had to be removed. So we would count the items in question together until we could remove the difference that existed.

That's what Jesus did: He removed the difference that existed between man who had been created and God who had created him. He has done away with the difference. Now there is no difference remaining to be reconciled between God and man.

That's why Jesus went forth to conquer! That's what He did in conquering! That's what we see represented in Revelation 6:2. Jesus is the One who conquered. He is the One who overcame. And because He overcame, we can, too.

We overcome, it says in Revelation 12:11, by the blood of the Lamb, and by the word of our testimony. Do we agree with what Jesus did? Yes, we do. Therefore, we possess what He did for us.

Opposition to the Plan of God

As we continue, we are going to open the other seals, and we will see immediate opposition, just as there was opposition to Jesus' ministry on the earth.

You will remember that the minute Jesus stood in the synagogue of His hometown of Nazareth and proclaimed that the Spirit of the Lord was upon Him, and "This day is this scripture fulfilled in your ears" (Luke 4:21), opposition arose. The devil began to fight Him, didn't he? We will see the same thing happen as the next seals are opened.

So far in Revelation chapter six, we have looked at the removal of *the first seal,* when Jesus went forth to do the work of Redemption.

Remember, we're seeing the Book of Revelation from God's perspective, and God sees everything as happening *now,* doesn't He?

Some will say, "Well, Jesus had already accomplished this work when John was caught away into heaven and saw his vision." That's right. It had already taken place. But the vast majority of what we will see under the seals had not yet been accomplished in John's time (although in God's point of view, it's all finished).

We are seeing things from God's point of view: We are seeing the work that Christ did, and we are also seeing the work of the enemy to try to stop it. But thank God, here in this sixth chapter, you're going to see that Satan can't stop it!

Again, if you have studied Church history, you might think he will succeed, because until now he has been successful in keeping the Church from completing the Great Commission. But in this sixth chapter and other passages you will find that the Church *will* successfully complete the task God gave it to do on the earth!

The Second Seal

We now come to *the second seal:*

And when he had opened the second seal, I heard the second beast say, Come and see.

And there went out another horse that was red: and power was given to him that sat thereon to take peace from the earth, and that they should kill one another: and there was given unto him a great sword.

Revelation 6:3,4

Again, living creatures are seen. Although we won't go into all the scriptures about this, *red symbolizes blood* and, in some cases, human suffering. (See Isaiah 1:18; Nahum 2:3; Isaiah 63:1,2.) Red symbolized this in the case of Jesus: He suffered and died, shedding His blood that we might be free. When we are washed in that blood, we are made as white as snow.

The color red symbolizes warfare that begins in the *spirit* realm and has an impact or effect in the earth in the *natural* realm. Thus, we understand that turmoil is going to come into the earth.

If you stop to think about it, in the first century, when Jesus did His work and the Church began, there was peace in the world. The Roman Empire had conquered most of the known world and had imposed a relatively peaceful reign (compared with what came before and afterwards) upon its subjects. It was called the *pax Romana:* Roman peace.

Constantine's Mixed Blessing

The Church, however, did not enjoy much peace during the first three hundred years of its existence. Much of this time, it was under heavy persecution by the Roman Empire. This changed around the year A.D. 300, when the Emperor Constantine had a vision of a heavenly cross and decided to force everyone in his empire to become a Christian — whether they wanted to be one or not. (Mandatory baptism doesn't make you a Christian, does it?)

Although Constantine's action gave the Church its first prolonged period of acceptance and peace, it ended up being a crushing blow that took the power out of the persecuted Church. The Church quickly conformed to the world, substituting wealth, power, prestige, and pagan practices for the power of God.

After the time of Constantine, the Roman Empire began to decay and fall apart. Barbarians, nomadic peoples who had no civilization like the Romans, broke through the borders and completely destroyed the western half of the Roman Empire. The eastern half continued in existence another thousand years, until the time of the Moslem conquest around A.D. 1300.

The peace that Rome had established was taken away. The first persecution of the Church had come through the Roman Empire; later it came at the hands of barbarians who fell upon the western empire and annihilated it. The barbarians also nearly destroyed the Early Church. They were totally opposed to it, because they were disinterested heathens — pagans.

So the Church dwindled in size and power for many reasons, including corruption from within its ranks and destruction from without. But the Lord had already told believers what was going to happen in the future!

The Church Shirks Its Responsibility

This rider on the red horse was given power to take peace from the earth. Who gave him this power? Was it God? No, God states clearly in His Word that His will is that there be peace on earth and goodwill to men (that's what He spoke by the angels at the birth of Christ). Furthermore, we are told in First Timothy 2 to pray for peace:

> **I exhort therefore, that, first of all, supplications, prayers, intercessions, and giving of thanks, be made for all men;**

> **For kings, and for all that are in authority; that we may lead a quiet and peaceable life in all godliness and honesty.**
>
> **For this is good and acceptable in the sight of God our Saviour;**
>
> **Who will have all men to be saved, and to come unto the knowledge of the truth.**
>
> **1 Timothy 2:1-4**

So whose *responsibility* is it that there be peace on earth? It's the Church's responsibility! That doesn't mean the whole earth will lie in peace at once, but it's up to those who believe to pray for peace so that the Gospel can be preached and men can have an opportunity to hear it. It's difficult to preach when bombs are exploding and bullets are flying, isn't it? No one wants to come to your meeting then!

We see in verse four, above, that is the will of God that all men everywhere be saved — but they're not, are they? It's because they haven't been given an opportunity to hear the Word (which they may then accept or reject).

So who gave the rider the ability to take peace from the earth? The Church did! How? By failing to do what God told it to do here in First Timothy. If we're told to pray for peace and we do, we will have it. Conversely, if we don't, it won't come!

That first century Church was vital: They knew how to pray! Do you remember what happened in Acts 4:31 when they prayed? The place where they met was shaken, and they went out and proclaimed the Gospel boldly, in spite of the persecution. *Persecution* never stops the Church, by the way. All it does is fan the fires of revival hotter.

The Ultimate Weapon Against the Church

What stops the Church? The same thing that effectively stopped the Early Church: *infiltration by the enemy*! Infiltration is the work of the devil.

Paul, Peter, and John warned the churches repeatedly in their writings that evil people would follow in their wake, teaching false doctrines. (And some of these false teachers would rise out of their own company, they said.)

False teachers *add onto the simple Gospel message* and get people over into areas like works instead of faith. The Bible says, "For by *grace* are ye saved *through faith; and that not of yourselves: it is the gift of God: Not of works,* lest any man should boast" (Ephesians 2:8,9). Nothing more than that!

But Gnostic teachers came along and added all kinds of requirements which they said you had to do or you wouldn't be saved. (There are still Gnostic teachers around today — even within the Charismatic Movement!)

I was running a ministry in California when members of a cult started to infiltrate our meetings. At first, half a dozen or so attended the midweek service. Then they started coming to Sunday meetings. After about three weeks, they began to stand up to testify. They'd say things like, "We rebuke the devil in this place, and we claim this place. . ."

After a few such "testimonies," I tried to talk to them, but they didn't want to talk. Finally I had to ask the sheriff to expel them, and then I had to get a restraining order to keep them off our property!

Before things got that far, one did talk to me. I asked him, "Do you believe that you're saved through faith in Jesus Christ and His blood?"

"Yeah, we do, *plus certain doctrines.*"

"Well, what are those?"

"Well, we can't tell you until you join us."

Gnostics are still trying to get into the Body of Christ. They are trying to destroy the fact that you are saved by grace, through the operation of faith. They are trying to take that away by adding other things.

God's anger is against people who add to or take away from the Gospel, according to Revelation 22:18: "For I testify unto every man that heareth the words of the prophecy of this book, If any man shall add unto these things, God shall add unto him the plagues that are written in this book."

Now, the first century Church was warned repeatedly not to tolerate Gnosticism. In fact, whole epistles were written to warn the churches not to tolerate Gnostics in their midst. Jesus Himself said in the beginning of Revelation, "Don't tolerate those things" (Revelation 2:15,16).

Why? Because false teachings and false doctrines will suck the very life out of the Church. And eventually they did! That's how the Early Church was weakened from within.

The devil attacked it from without over and over again, but he couldn't weaken it. Attacking the Church from the *outside* does not weaken it; it does just the opposite. But when you attack from *within* with false teachings and false doctrines, it weakens the Church.

I was born and reared in a denomination that had been so weakened by false doctrines that it was hardly recognizable as Christian. Thank God, that denomination has been revived and is coming back to where it belongs, but for a period of fifty or sixty years, it was ruled by head knowledge instead of heart knowledge.

We are to take our dominion and war in the spirit to keep peace on this earth. No, the whole earth will not be engulfed in peace before Jesus comes, and we're not here to accomplish that. We're here to preach the Gospel to every creature, and we are to pray against wars and rumors of war.

God's Promises for Lebanon

For example, we need to pray for war-torn Lebanon which, until 1976, was the most beautiful part of the Middle East. We need to stand on God's promises to Lebanon and pray for peace in that nation so the Gospel may go forth freely into all the factions who live there — Moslems, Druse, Christians, and others.

God's promises to Lebanon are found in Isaiah 29:

Is it not yet a very little while, and Lebanon shall be turned into a fruitful field, and the fruitful field shall be esteemed as a forest?

And in that day shall the deaf hear the words of the book, and the eyes of the blind shall see out of obscurity, and out of darkness.

The meek also shall increase their joy in the Lord, and the poor among men shall rejoice in the Holy One of Israel.

For the terrible one is brought to nought, and the scorner is consumed, and all that watch for iniquity are cut off.

Isaiah 29:17-20

We can stand on those promises and pray for peace in Lebanon. It's *our* responsibility, not God's, to change the situation there. You can't just say, "O God, change that place over there." No, you must pray for peace like

God told you to. Then God can do something: He'll send forth angels, and they will change the situation.

You see, *prayer is just as important a part of the Great Commission as going to a foreign land.* In fact, if you go without prayer, you will be sorely disappointed. You need prayers of all kinds when you go to places that have been dominated by other spirits for hundreds or even thousands of years.

Intercession must be made before you go, and you must have prayer support behind you once you're there. Of course, you need to pray, too. Then you'll be free to fulfill the ministry God has given you in those places, and the people will be free to receive it.

The Results of Intercession in India

In 1983, I preached in Madras, India, in a Rhema World Outreach Seminar. Two thousand ministers came from all over India — north to south — and even beyond its borders. I never saw a more rapt, attentive audience anywhere.

Those ministers came from every kind of Christian background you can think of, but they never argued with what we taught. They just sat there and drained us. They took in everything we had, and more than we knew we had, all day long for seven days.

We would start at 8 o'clock in the morning and we wouldn't finish until 11 o'clock at night — and they didn't want to stop then! Neither did they want to break for lunch after sitting through a three-hour morning session. The second session lasted all afternoon in 100-degree heat outdoors, and we Americans were the only ones the heat fazed.

At this time, we also preached a crusade in a Hindu shrine city that had a population of 140,000 people. This city had never had a Christian meeting in its long history — not one! That's hard for us to believe, because we live in a country where the Word of God has been sown and reaped and sown and reaped many times, even in small towns, but there are few Christians in India, percentage wise.

The Indian brother who helped us organize the Outreach said, "I've been praying for that city for 26 years. I've been believing God for 26 years that we would have a meeting there." Until then, the authorities had refused permission.

Team member Jerry O'Dell preached a very simple Gospel message: "God loves you. God sent Jesus to show His love. Jesus died so you could have life. Now you can receive it." And the people did!

People who were maimed were restored. People who were blind, saw. People who were deaf, heard. People who were crippled, walked. Demon-possessed people crawling on the ground like snakes were set free! And multitudes accepted Jesus as their Savior.

Hindus Testify

A 75-year-old Hindu priest wearing an orange robe came out of the crowd one night to testify, "My ears just opened!"

He hadn't heard anything for 15 years. He couldn't hear Jerry preach, but he came to the meeting anyway. And standing in the presence of God, God spoke to his spirit, "Listen to this man!" Then his ears popped open, he listened to the message, and he accepted Jesus!

He said, "I've been a Hindu priest all my life. I was raised to be one. Tonight Jesus opened my ears and I heard the Gospel. And I received Him as my Lord, the

One and only Living God! Now the state won't pay me anymore, but God will take care of me." (In India, the state pays a salary to Hindu priests.)

Another man stood up to testify. He was about 55 years old. He said, "I've been a Hindu all my life. Tonight I received Jesus Christ as my Lord and Savior, and I've been delivered from poverty." Jerry hadn't said anything about poverty in his message; he had said that Jesus wants to save, heal, and deliver people. How did that man know he had been delivered from poverty? The Spirit of God told him!

The success of this crusade came about because a group of people at Rhema Bible Church had prayed for us for several months before we left, and while we were in India they continued to pray.

As you walk around Madras and other Indian cities, you will sense demonic infestation in a moment, if you have any spiritual discernment at all. There are many evidences of the devil's activities, even in the natural. This was especially true in Chidambaram, the Hindu city where we held the crusade. The heaviness of demonic oppression was present all the time.

However, when it was time for our meeting, a host of angels came to our aid, and the whole atmosphere changed instantly! The place was charged with faith, hope, and love, and the Indian people were able to receive what was being preached. They were not hindered by centuries of demonic bondage. They were free! They could hear! They could respond to God! And they did!

So many were saved, we left two Indian brothers behind in that city to begin a church and pastor it. We took an offering which enabled them to buy a building and two bicycles (which was like giving them two automobiles). These two brothers had been trained in Brother Sam Chelludurai's school, and he said, "They are ready. Leave them here." And they are still there, pastoring those people.

God will do wonderful things like this if we'll do our part. Our part begins with praying to keep peace in the earth and to open doors that have been closed to the Gospel.

Because this infiltrated Church did not live up to its responsibilities in prayer in these areas, *the second seal* was opened, and "power was given to him. . .to take peace from the earth, and that they should kill one another: and there was given unto him a great sword" (Revelation 6:4). This sword would wage war in the earth in both the natural and spiritual realms.

The Third Seal

Then John saw *the third seal* opened:

> **And when he had opened the third seal, I heard the third beast say, Come and see. And I beheld, and lo a black horse; and he that sat on him had a pair of balances in his hand.**
>
> **Revelation 6:5**

Black symbolizes judgment, and the horse once again symbolizes warfare. Several scriptures will show us this.

First, let's look at Lamentations 4:7 and 8:

> **Her Nazarites were purer than snow, they were whiter than milk, they were more ruddy in body than rubies, their polishing was of sapphire:**
>
> **Their visage is blacker than a coal; they are not known in the streets: their skin cleaveth to their bones; it is withered, it is become like a stick.**

In other words, judgment has come upon that which was once in order with God. It got out of order by disobedience, so judgment has come upon it. We just saw that the rider of the black horse in Revelation 6:5 was holding a pair of balances. These balances, or scales, symbolize justice and judgment: God will weigh things in the balance.

Verse six reads, "And I heard a voice in the midst of the four beasts say, A measure of wheat for a penny, and three measures of barley for a penny. . . ."

A penny was generally considered a day's wage in New Testament times. Thus, it would take two days' wages to purchase a loaf of bread made of wheat and barley. In other words, the voice was predicting a time of famine.

What kind of famine emerges first, before natural famine? Spiritual famine. The verse concludes, ". . . see thou hurt not the oil and the wine." This is the good news, and it is addressed to those who know God and are walking in the truth. Oil symbolizes what? The Holy Spirit. Wine symbolizes what? The blood of Jesus.

In other words, those who have been bought by the blood and are walking in the Spirit — controlled by and helped by Him — are not defeated by such things as famines. They never have been, and they never will be.

Another scriptural account of famine is found in the Book of Joel. The prophet describes natural famine in chapter one:

> That which the palmerworm hath left hath the locust eaten; and that which the locust hath left hath the cankerworm eaten; and that which the cankerworm hath left hath the caterpiller eaten. . . .

> For a nation is come up upon my land, strong, and
> without number, whose teeth are the teeth of a lion,
> and he hath the cheek teeth of a great lion.
>
> **Joel 1:4,6**

Famine has come upon Israel in the natural! Later on in Joel we will find spiritual famine and restoration described.

Famine is also described unmistakably in the Book of Nahum. Nahum was the second prophet whom God sent to the Assyrian city of Ninevah. Jonah, the first, didn't want to go, but being swallowed by "the great fish" changed his mind. And when Jonah preached, the whole city listened — and repented!

But now, 150 years later, the people have returned to their old ways, so God has sent another prophet, Nahum, to them.

Nahum said, "She is empty, and void, and waste: and the heart melteth, and the knees smite together, and much pain is in all loins, and the faces of them all gather blackness" (Nahum 2:10).

This describes judgment on a people who didn't accept the word of the Lord. Because the people of Ninevah rejected Nahum's message, God sent judgment upon the Assyrian nation and it was destroyed.

A Famine Not of Bread

God did not send famine capriciously, for no reason. Natural and/or spiritual famines occur when people disobey God's Word to them, as we see in Amos 8: "Behold, the days come, saith the Lord God, that I will send a famine in the land, not a famine of bread, nor a thirst for water, but of hearing the words of the Lord" (v. 11).

77

God said, "If you believe me — if you trust Me — I'll bless you." He told the people in the Old and New Testaments (and He tells us today), "Whatsoever a man soweth, that shall he also reap." And He said, "In that day, if you don't trust Me — if you don't believe Me — you will bring all those curses upon yourself." This is a picture of what happened when Israel didn't believe God.

Amos spoke of a famine not of bread or water, "but of hearing the words of the Lord." He continues, "And they shall wander from sea to sea, and from the north even to the east, they shall run to and fro to seek the word of the Lord, and shall not find it. In that day shall the fair virgins and young men faint for thirst" (vv. 12,13). So they do — but why? Because the leaders and the nation of Israel didn't obey Him.

What is happening in the world today is because believers through the centuries did not pray and do what they should or could have done to fulfill the Great Commission.

I do not wish to sound overly critical of previous generations of believers, however. If these people had not obeyed God to the extent they did, we would not be where we are in terms of spiritual growth today. Many times of refreshing from the presence of the Lord have come through various saints during different times. Thank God for all of them!

However, there is a famine for hearing the words of the Lord still today. Some people on earth are starving for the Word of God and can't find it!

Consider the set of balances we saw in Revelation 6. We have been weighed in the balance and found wanting! Judgment has come upon the Church in many ways. That plague of locusts that Joel spoke of has invaded the Church and eaten up the good things. *The Bread of Life is missing!*

Jesus said, "I am the bread." When the Bread is missing, spiritual famine will result — and natural famine may follow. (Natural famine is a result of spiritual famine, not the other way around, as we saw earlier.)

". . .see thou hurt not the oil and the wine," we read. In other words, hurt not those who have been saved. Those who have walked in the Spirit and in the truth are not defeated by such things as famine.

What did Jesus say in Luke 10:19? "Nothing shall by any means hurt you." He was addressing His own disciples, and He told them, "Go out there and do what I tell you to do, and nothing by any means shall hurt you." "Nothing" is a big subject. "Nothing shall by any means hurt you."

As we have discussed before, there has always been a remnant who believed God, even if the rest of the world lay in darkness. Remember Elijah's day? Elijah at one point grumbled that he was the only person left who believed in God, and he wished he were dead. Sometimes you may be tempted to think you're all alone, too, but don't get discouraged; God has many believers.

Remember what God said to Elijah? "I've got seven thousand more just like you, Elijah, who have not bowed their knee to Baal." There's always a remnant, and today there are many more than a remnant. Thank God, we're living in a time of great harvest.

The Fourth Seal

There is another horse we need to look at in Revelation 6:

> And when he had opened the fourth seal, I heard the voice of the fourth beast say, Come and see.
>
> And I looked, and behold a pale horse: and his name that sat on him was Death, and Hell followed with him. And Power was given unto them over the fourth part of the earth, to kill with sword, and with hunger, and with death, and with the beasts of the earth.

Revelation 6:7,8

The pale horse symbolizes death and warfare, for *paleness symbolizes death*, and the horse symbolizes warfare. Again, who gave death and hell power over the fourth part of the earth? The Church, by not praying and taking the dominion or authority it possesses, and by not preaching the Gospel to the degree that it was commissioned to do.

Death and hell were given power "to kill with sword, and with hunger, and with death, and with the beasts of the earth."

Again, we see both symbolic and natural meaning here. Symbolically, these "beasts" are spirit beings! The Greek word used to describe them — *therion* — means "dangerous, poisonous, venomous, evil creatures." It is an entirely different word from the word used in chapter four for "living creature" — *zoon*.

All kinds of deaths are symbolized here in chapter six — spiritual as well as natural: the sword, hunger and famine, death, and the beasts these forces rule in a wicked way.

Just think of the men manipulated by evil spirits throughout history who have deceived other people and plunged them into darkness — and eventually death: Attila the Hun, Genghis Khan, Mohammed, Hitler, and Stalin. Men like them cruelly defeated other peoples by shedding vast amounts of blood. Men like them have afflicted a fourth part of the earth, the verse says.

The Fifth Seal

> **And when he had opened the fifth seal, I saw under the altar the souls of them that were slain for the word of God, and for the testimony which they held:**
>
> **And they cried with a loud voice, saying, How long, O Lord, holy and true, dost thou not judge and avenge our blood on them that dwell on the earth?**
>
> **And white robes were given unto every one of them; and it was said unto them, that they should rest yet for a little season, until their fellowservants also and their brethren, that should be killed as they were, should be fulfilled.**
>
> **Revelation 6:9-11**

John is discussing martyrdom and natural death here. He is saying that there will be martyrs until the end of the age, and that many will be persecuted and die because they believe on Jesus Christ. (I will cover the subject of martyrdom in Volume 2 of this series.)

The passage says that those who are under the altar are crying out for vengeance. I once heard a minister preach on this verse. He said those souls under the altar are Jews who have gone to heaven but are not saved yet, and they are crying out for vengeance. But no one goes to heaven without being saved.

Another theory is that these are souls who are not repentant enough yet. No! There isn't any carnality in heaven. We need to get our whole mind renewed now, in this world.

What, then, is crying out for vengeance? It is blood that was shed unjustly. What did the blood of righteous

Abel do? It cried out to God for vengeance. And God, being just, heard it. He asked Cain, "What hast thou done? the voice of thy brother's blood crieth unto me from the ground" (Genesis 4:10). You don't hear the voice of that blood with your ears, but God hears it.

Jesus' blood speaks, too, doesn't it? The Bible says it speaks *better* things than the blood of Abel (Hebrews 12:24). It speaks *life!* Praise God, our sins are washed in Jesus' blood, and we have abundant life because of it. Through the blood of Jesus we also have deliverance, safety, preservation, and everything else we need in this world.

Those under the altar crying out for vengeance are partly a picture of what happened because believers did not exercise the dominion or authority that was given to the Church. The result was death to innocent people and those believers being semi-defeated and in turmoil.

The Church, however, has never been totally defeated, because there has always been a remnant — the oil and the wine — who believed God and were not hurt by this. (Again, refer to my section on martyrdom in Volume 2, which is forthcoming.)

Chapter 8
The Victorious Church in the Age of Grace

So far in this sixth chapter of Revelation, we've been looking at the beginning of the Age of Grace. We've seen the beginning of the work that Jesus did, and we've seen what the devil did to try to stop it.

In one instance, the devil tried to kill Jesus at the hands of an angry mob in Nazareth (Luke 4). But because Jesus was manifesting the glory of God, no harm came to Him. That fact should be comforting to you and me. The same protection will be yours when you are manifesting God's glory. The glory will keep you. It will protect you.

In the sixth chapter of Revelation, we've also seen how the Church missed it through the centuries. But now we're going to see where the Church makes it! You may say, "Well, it certainly doesn't sound like it when you read it." No? Well, just wait a minute!

What we are looking at here is the Age of the Church. We saw how the Church started with a bang in the first century. Then we saw how the devil infiltrated it and weakened it until it became ineffectual in the earth.

We saw how the Church partially failed to complete its mission of world evangelization — until now. But now we are going to see the rest of this story. From here on, we will see an overcoming and victorious Church!

The Sixth Seal

And I beheld when he had opened the sixth seal, and, lo, there was a great earthquake; and the sun became black as sackcloth of hair, and the moon became as blood.

Revelation 6:12

All the way through the Old and New Testaments, earthquakes have often accompanied great acts of faith. In other words, earthquakes have accompanied "earth-shaking events" — events that have changed things for the better spiritually in this earth.

One such act of faith occurred in the Old Testament when King Saul's son Jonathan and his armorbearer finally got tired of hiding and decided to go out and challenge the Philistine invaders. Saul and his men remained safely behind the lines, unaware of what Jonathan was planning.

Mountain-Moving Faith

Jonathan said, "We'll walk up to them and show ourselves to them. If they say, 'Come up here,' that will be a sign to us that God has delivered them into our hands." (That's faith, isn't it?)

The Philistines saw them and said, "Look at the Israelites coming out of their holes. Come up here, and we'll make bread out of you." So up they went. The terrain was so steep and rocky, they had to crawl on their hands and knees to reach this great host of Philistines that had invaded their land.

After they killed about twenty Philistines, something happened: an earthquake! It says in First Samuel 14:15, "...the earth quaked: so it was a very great trembling."

God shook the earth and put such fear in the hearts of the Philistine host, they turned and fled before Jonathan and his armorbearer. Just two Israelites chased the whole Philistine army out of the land of Israel! It was that act of faith of Jonathan that brought about the earthquake. (Not every earthquake is caused because someone is in faith, however.)

Before studying the most significant earthquake that ever occurred, we will read Revelation 6:12-14 as background.

> And I beheld when he had opened the sixth seal, and, lo, there was a great earthquake; and the sun became black as sackcloth of hair, and the moon became as blood;
>
> And the stars of heaven fell unto the earth, even as a fig tree casteth her untimely figs, when she is shaken of a mighty wind.
>
> And the heaven departed as a scroll when it is rolled together; and every mountain and island were moved out of their places.

The most significant earthquake in history occurred on the day of Jesus' Crucifixion, at the moment when His spirit and soul left His body:

> Jesus, when he had cried again with a loud voice, yielded up the ghost.
>
> And, behold, the veil of the temple was rent in twain from the top to the bottom; and the earth did quake, and the rocks rent.
>
> Matthew 27:50,51

The Crucifixion was an earth-shaking event, wasn't it? It says in First Corinthians that if Satan and his forces had known how much the Crucifixion would change things for the better on this earth, they wouldn't have crucified Jesus!

> But we speak the wisdom of God in a mystery, even the hidden wisdom, which God ordained before the world unto our glory:
>
> Which none of the princes of this world knew: for had they known it, they would not have crucified the Lord of glory.

> **1 Corinthians 2:7,8**

But there is another earthquake connected with this event, according to Matthew 28:

> In the end of the sabbath, as it began to dawn toward the first day of the week, came Mary Magdalene and the other Mary to see the sepulchre.
>
> And, behold, there was a great earthquake: for the angel of the Lord descended from heaven, and came and rolled back the stone from the door, and sat upon it.

> **Matthew 28:1,2**

The women went to see the sepulchre, where Jesus' body had been placed. "And, behold, there was a great earthquake." This earthquake marked His Resurrection! Do you think Jesus' Resurrection changed things for the better? It certainly did: Faith was producing its effect in the earth!

We have now seen that an earthquake often does accompany unusual moves of God. Our background text for this study was Revelation 6:12-14, which spoke of a great earthquake occurring when the sixth seal was opened; and accompanying the earthquake, "...the sun became black as sackcloth of hair, and the moon became as blood."

Many have tried to put a natural interpretation on this verse. Sometimes you can put a natural interpretation on things that will happen to the sun, moon, and stars, but I don't believe you can with Revelation 6:12.

Just think about it: In the natural realm, if the sun were darkened, the moon would also be darkened. It is the lesser light; all it does is reflect sunlight. If the sun were darkened, that wouldn't make the moon red.

Joel 1: The Harvest Is Devoured

To understand this correctly, we must turn to the first chapter of the Book of Joel. Joel was one of the prophets whom God used mightily to minister to the nation of Israel.

> **Hear this, ye old men, and give ear, all ye inhabitants of the land. Hath this been in your days, or even in the days of your fathers?**
>
> **Joel 1:2**

Bear in mind that Joel, living in the days of the Old Covenant, is prophesying to Israel about the future of that nation. Bear in mind, too, that prophecies like this in the Old Testament are subject to at least three different interpretations:

1. The writer is addressing exactly whom he says he is addressing; furthermore, the meaning is *exactly* what he says it is. In other words, when he's talking about Israel, he means Israel.

2. The writer is addressing the people he names — but he is also addressing other nations and/or believers in the Church today. In other words, his meaning is *symbolic.*

Old Testament prophecies will not necessarily apply to the Church line upon line and precept upon precept; however, there are things that God wants the Church to see in these prophecies.

For example, in First Corinthians 10:11, Paul writes of the nation of Israel, "Now all these things happened unto them [under the Old Testament] for ensamples: and they are written for our admonition [under the New Testament], upon whom the ends of the world are come."

3. In the Spirit, you and I can receive *personal* truths relating to us from a passage. God speaks to us individually out of His Word, doesn't He?

These meanings will become clearer to you as you see what God is saying in Joel to the nation of Israel, to the Church, and to you yourself.

> **Tell ye your children of it, and let your children tell their children, and their children another generation.**
>
> **That which the palmerworm hath left hath the locust eaten; and that which the locust hath left hath the cankerworm eaten; and that which the cankerworm hath left hath the caterpiller eaten.**
>
> **Joel 1:3,4**

What do palmerworms, locusts, cankerworms, and caterpillars do? *They destroy the harvest!* They don't come and eat the immature plants that are just shooting out of the ground. They wait until the harvest is ready; then they come and consume it right down to the ground.

The Husbandman Waiteth

God meant for there to be a harvest in every generation. God intended and provided a harvest for Himself every year since the cross. Even though God's harvest has repeatedly been devoured, James 5:7 tells us that the Lord has great patience for this harvest:

> ...Behold, the husbandman waiteth for the
> precious fruit of the earth, and hath long patience for
> it, until he receive the early and latter rain.

The "fruit" God is waiting for is not apples, oranges, and bananas. It's the lives of "just men made perfect" — souls — that's what He is waiting for!

We see in Israel's harvests the "type," or symbol of what the Church is experiencing today. Their natural harvest was devoured when the children of Israel were disobedient. The former and the latter rains did not fall. The harvest was lost for lack of productivity. Then the insects would arrive and devour what little was left.

So the palmerworms, locusts, cankerworms, and caterpillars represent disobedience, sin, tradition, and unbelief. *These things eat up the harvest that God had provided for Himself.* And it has been eaten up for ages and ages.

As we studied earlier, there would be a famine for the Word of God. Men would even run to and fro looking for it, but they couldn't find it.

Let's look further at Joel's prophecy:

> Awake, ye drunkards, and weep; and howl, all ye
> drinkers of wine, because of the new wine; for it is
> cut off from your mouth.
>
> For a nation is come up upon my land, strong, and
> without number, whose teeth are the teeth of a lion,
> and he hath the cheek teeth of a great lion.
>
> He hath laid my vine waste, and barked my fig
> tree: he hath made it clean bare, and cast it away; the
> branches thereof are made white.

> Joel 1:5-7

Israel was God's vine — and Israel was laid waste in Joel's time. The expression "he hath barked my fig tree" is also representative of Israel just prior to their captivity. You can see from these verses that the fruit is taken away from them. Symbolically, then, we can also see where the Church has missed it and failed to harvest all it could have.

In verse 11, God tells Israel (and the Church):

> Be ye ashamed, O ye husbandmen; howl, O ye vinedressers, for the wheat and for the barley; because the harvest of the field is perished.

God always likens the winning of the lost to harvesting. For example, in John 4:35, Jesus told his disciples, "Lift up your eyes, and look on the fields; for they are white already to harvest." And in Matthew 9:37,38, He said, "The harvest truly is plenteous, but the labourers are few; Pray ye therefore the Lord of the harvest, that he will send forth labourers into his harvest."

In this passage in Joel, God is saying that the harvest has been lost. It has perished.

> The vine is dried up, and the fig tree languisheth; the pomegranate tree, the palm tree also, and the apple tree, even all the trees of the field, are withered: because joy is withered away from the sons of men.
>
> Joel 1:12

Throughout the scriptures, you will find that *trees symbolize people.* In this verse, God says that all of these trees are dry. Have you ever been to a church service that wasn't very lively? What did you call it? *Dry!* It didn't do you much good, did it? So the dryness of the Church is what has caused the loss of this harvest, just as the dryness of Israel's spiritual condition — disobedience — caused the loss of its natural harvest.

As we saw, the insects represent the things that caused us to miss it. We've sinned. We've gotten into unbelief. We've substituted man's traditions for the

Word of God. We've been disobedient to God. Now He tells us how to deal with this situation:

Sanctify ye a fast, call a solemn assembly, gather the elders and all the inhabitants of the land into the house of the Lord your God, and cry unto the Lord.

Alas for the day! for the day of the Lord is at hand, and as a destruction from the Almighty shall it come.

Joel 1:14,15

Joel 2: A Call to Repentance

The second chapter of Joel opens with the words, "Blow ye the trumpet in Zion...." We sing those words all the time. But where is Zion? *Zion is the Church!* It's those who believe God.

"Blow ye the trumpet in Zion, and sound an alarm in my holy mountain...." *God's holy mountain is the kingdom of heaven.* This first verse concludes, "let all the inhabitants of the land tremble: for the day of the Lord cometh, for it is nigh at hand."

In verses that follow, God tells us more of what will happen. He warns us and calls us to repent. He tells us to dedicate and commit ourselves to fulfill His will in the earth:

Blow the trumpet in Zion, sanctify a fast, call a solemn assembly:

Gather the people, sanctify the congregation, assemble the elders, gather the children, and those that suck the breasts: let the bridegroom go forth of his chamber, and the bride out of her closet.

Joel 2:15,16

This describes people of all ages and walks of life. It's a call to start majoring in majors instead of minors; to start concentrating on things of eternal value instead of concentrating on things of fleeting, earthly interest. Then God starts talking to you and me:

> **Let the priests, the ministers of the Lord, weep between the porch and the altar, and let them say, Spare thy people, O Lord, and give not thine heritage to reproach, that the heathen should rule over them: wherefore should they say among the people, Where is their God?**
>
> **Joel 2:17**

Every member of the Body of Christ has the ministry of reconciliation (2 Corinthians 5:18). Also, God said in Psalm 2:8, "Ask of me, and I shall give thee the heathen for thine inheritance...." However, if we as members of the Body of Christ do not fortify ourselves and then go forth in that strength to do the work that God gave us to do to win the lost, it isn't going to be done! That's what He is saying here.

We need to repent first, don't we? We the saved — not some unsaved person somewhere — need to repent. When we, the priests and ministers of the Lord, repent, pray, and take hold of this burden of God for the lost, getting into agreement with God about it, what will happen? Our repentance and intercession for the lost will pave the way for world revival and harvest!

> **Then will the Lord be jealous for his land, and pity his people.**
>
> **Yea, the Lord will answer and say unto his people, Behold, I will send you corn, and wine, and oil, and ye shall be satisfied therewith: and I will no more make you a reproach among the heathen.**
>
> **Joel 2:18,19**

The Promises of the Harvest

Let's examine these verses. God said, "I will send you corn, and wine, and oil, and ye shall be satisfied therewith...." When we understand and participate in God's heart toward harvesting the world, He will send us corn, wine, and oil — things that will deeply satisfy the longings of our hearts.

In that age, bread was made out of corn or various grains. Thus, the word "corn" could easily be thought of as "wheat." It would mean the same thing; it has the same impact.

Corn symbolizes the Word of God. So when God said, "I will send you corn," it means He will send us the Bread of Life, hallelujah! He said He would do this *after* we repent. Isn't He dealing with us to repent right now? Thank God, He is.

Wine symbolizes the blood of Jesus Christ. This life-giving blood still flows continually from Calvary. Blood also symbolizes the joy of the Lord.

Oil symbolizes the work of the Holy Spirit. Jesus promised He would send us the Comforter, the Holy Spirit, to fill us.

God promised that the corn, wine, and oil would satisfy us, and we would no longer be a reproach. His promises continue in verses 21 and 22:

> **Fear not, O land; be glad and rejoice: for the Lord will do great things.**
>
> **Be not afraid, ye beasts of the field: for the pastures of the wilderness do spring, for the tree beareth her fruit, the fig tree and the vine do yield their strength.**

This means there will be a revival — a life-giving time! The vine and the fig tree that were barked and made clean and white, and had no fruit on them, will be fruitful again.

> **Be glad then, ye children of Zion, and rejoice in the Lord your God: for he hath given you the former rain moderately, and he will cause to come down for you the rain, the former rain, and the latter rain in the first month.**

> And the floors shall be full of wheat, and the fats [vats] shall overflow with wine and oil.
>
> Joel 2:23,24

What is the floor used for? That's where you put the harvest! What is a vat (translated as "fat" here in the *King James Version*)? That's where you put the harvest in a hole in the ground.

The Former and the Latter Rain

God also said He would give us rain. *Rain symbolizes the working of the Holy Spirit.* The "former rain" has been coming moderately in wave after wave. Even before the Pentecostal revival, God used great evangelists like Charles Finney, Dwight L. Moody, the Wesleys, and others to stir the Church into revivals.

Revivals have burst forth sporadically through the centuries, ever since Martin Luther recognized that justification is by faith, not by works. Wave after wave of revivals have come and gone, representing "the former rain moderately." Unfortunately, these revivals often were infiltrated by the devil, just like he infiltrated the Church in the first few centuries.

In this century, we have seen revivals occur in the following progression: the Pentecostal Movement, the Latter Rain Movement, the Charismatic Movement, and this Word Movement, which I do not think will cease. So the Church has come out of its dead period, where it was working the works of the flesh to attain salvation, and it has come back into the light of God.

God knows the future, and He is faithful to tell His children what will happen in the future. He wants you to know *exactly* what He is going to do here in the earth — just as He told His friend Abraham in the time of the patriarchs. (Remember, Jesus called us His friends, too!)

It is implied in Genesis 18:16-19 that two angels were discussing whether or not to warn Abraham about the coming destruction of Sodom and Gomorrah. The Lord replied, "Shall I hide from Abraham that thing which I do" (Genesis 18:17).

The Lord then told Abraham that He was planning to destroy those cities because "their sin is very grievous" (v. 20). Abraham interceded with the Lord on behalf of the righteous inhabitants, and the Lord finally promised to spare Sodom if He could find only ten righteous people in all the city. (When He couldn't, the city was destroyed!)

God wants *you* to know what He's doing in the earth, too. God spent thirty-seven percent of the Bible telling you that. That's why I believe that it is worthwhile to read the Book of Joel.

I would hate to get to heaven, be walking down one of its golden streets, run into Joel, and hear him ask, "Did you read my letter," and my only response could be, "What letter?"

The Book of Joel is addressed to you and me, upon whom the ends of the world are come, to teach, admonish, and instruct us. On the Day of Pentecost, Peter said, "This is that which was spoken by the prophet Joel" (Acts 2:16).

God's Plan for a Quick Harvest

In Joel 2, God said that He has given us the former rain moderately. The good news is that He'll send us both the former rain and the latter rain in the first month (v. 23).

The *former rain* came to Israel after the harvest and after the fields had lain idle for a period of time. The former rain came to prepare the ground to receive the seed — to soften it — to give it what it needed to be fruitful. It fell before the planting.

The *latter rain* fell between the planting and the harvest — during the growing season — so there would be a full harvest.

Several years ago, a farmer in my Bible class got up and taught us about the importance of water to a harvest. I've never forgotten his illustration.

He held up two ears of corn from the same field. The long, full, fruitful ear came from the center of the field, which had been irrigated during the growing season. The short ear, which only had a few kernels, came from a corner which the irrigation system missed. (It didn't get the latter rain!)

That's a picture of what the Church has been doing throughout the centuries. Although it has been harvesting, it has never harvested the abundant crop it should have. For one thing, it didn't go into the harvest field using all the equipment God gave it. It didn't go out in the full power of the Holy Spirit, which is the latter rain!

God can't fully bless works which are done largely in the flesh. To bring in the full harvest, we must work in the Holy Spirit and be controlled by the Spirit.

Usually six months or more separated the former and the latter rains in Israel. But God said in the time of the end, the two rains would occur close together. Remember, the former rain makes the ground able to receive the seed, and the latter rain produces the full harvest.

I saw this happen in front of my own eyes during my missionary trip to India. In that pagan city where no one had ever heard the Word of God preached, the Word went into that "ground" of the people's hearts and produced an instant harvest of souls! We had the former and latter rain close together — "in the first month."

God says in Romans 9 that He will do a quick work upon the earth, which is what Isaiah prophesied:

> Esaias also crieth concerning Israel, Though the number of the children of Israel be as the sand of the sea, a remnant shall be saved:
>
> For he will finish the work, and cut it short in righteousness: because a short work will the Lord make upon the earth.
>
> And as Esaias said before, Except the Lord of Sabaoth had left us a seed, we had been as Sodoma, and been made like unto Gomorrha.
>
> Romans 9:27-29

The population of the earth presently stands at 5 billion persons. God has raised this huge population up for *Himself*, not for the devil! As of about 1890, the world's population was only one billion. By 1948, there were two billion. In 1980 we reached 4 billion. At the present rate, there will be seven or eight billion by the year 2000, if the Lord tarries.

God did not make a mistake when He raised up this huge population! He has always known it would be here. He instructed Adam and Noah to populate the earth. (Some have said that's the only commandment of God that men have kept!)

Leaders in many branches of modern science, government, and industry worry about how the world is going to handle this huge population. Don't worry — God did this! God has raised up this harvest of billions of souls for Himself! He has long patience for the precious fruit of the earth!

The Overflowing Harvest

We have been told by the prophet Joel to expect the former rain and the latter rain in the first month. This will lead to such an overflowing harvest that the floors shall be full of wheat, and the vats shall overflow with wine and oil, which is the work that the blood of Jesus Christ has wrought and the Holy Spirit is providing.

The leaders of some churches are so afraid they are going to lose a few members; especially if a newcomer moves into town and starts another church.

When God's final harvest comes, these leaders are no longer going to be worried about losing a few members. Instead, they're going to be calling other pastors, pleading, "I've got hundreds more than I can handle. Can you take some of them off my hands? Just take a few hundred of my members. Please help me!"

Remember when Jesus told Peter in Luke 5:4, "Launch out into the deep, and let down your nets for a draught." The disciples did let down their empty nets — they had been fishing all night without success — and their nets broke under the weight of the catch.

What did the disciples do next? They beckoned to their partners on another ship, calling, "Come here. Help us." Luke tells us, "And they came, and filled both the ships, so that they began to sink." Peter and the others were astonished at the size of the catch. But Jesus said to Peter, "Fear not; from henceforth thou shalt catch men."

You're going to see this same thing happen in the last harvest. You're going to see church leaders looking around for help to handle all of the people who have been saved. (It's a lot of fun catching fish, but it's not so much fun cleaning them!)

The Coming Restoration

And I will restore to you the years that the locust hath eaten, the cankerworm, and the caterpiller, and the palmerworm, my great army which I sent among you.

Joel 2:25

This verse is the part of Joel's prophecy that thrills me the most, because I have seen it fulfilled in my own life. For years I saw the locust, the cankerworm, the caterpillar, and the palmerworm eat up my life — and not only my life, but my family's as well.

That devastation came upon Israel, and later the Church, because of their sin, disobedience, and failure to do what God had commanded them to do. That's why they lost the harvest.

But has God said, "Well, it's all over; there's nothing left to do"? No, God has a plan that works. He has shown us this plan throughout the Bible — not just in the Book of Joel. He promises, "I will restore to you the years that the locust hath eaten" — the harvest that was lost.

Starting with the first century, there have been many years in Church history when much of the harvest was lost, haven't there? Men were running to and fro. The Church was engaged in all kinds of things except what it should have been. And even in times of revival, the devil was busy counterattacking. He was successful primarily because of lack of teaching. People didn't hold on to what they had received in the revival as they should have.

But God has always known that it will take one wave building upon another, then another, and another, until finally there will be a wave that can't be defeated. And that is what is on the horizon now!

Amos Prophesies of Our Day

Do you want to see this in the Word? In Amos 9, we see a reference to the day in which we are living:

> **In that day will I raise up the tabernacle of David that is fallen, and close up the breaches thereof; and I will raise up his ruins, and I will build it as in the days of old.**
>
> **Amos 9:11**

When Amos prophesies about the tabernacle of David here, he is talking about the restoration that is coming in the Body of Christ. Didn't Peter preach in Acts 3 that there would be a restoration of all things that the prophets had said? He also said that Jesus would remain in heaven until that happened.

In the time of restoration, God said that He would raise up the tabernacle of David that had fallen. *The tabernacle symbolizes a place of continual praise and worship.* The tabernacle of David was open to the people twenty-four hours a day. The priests and levites ministered to God round the clock with singing, instrumental music, and loud praises.

The Ark of the Covenant was located right in the middle of God's people, inside the Holy Place. David had had a revelation from God about how it could be placed in the midst of the people without causing their destruction: He just put it in a tent. As long as the ark was served in the way God showed David, the presence of God blessed the people.

The Tabernacle of Moses, on the other hand, was still in existence in Gibeon. In fact, the priests were still performing the service of that tabernacle *without the ark in the Holy of Holies.* Anyone who wanted to, could go to Gibeon and still perform the rituals, even though the actual ark of God was right there among the people in Jerusalem! (Does that remind you of anything you see today?)

The ark was symbolic of the presence of God. God wanted to be there among His people. Then, as now, God dwelt in the praises of His people (Psalm 22:3).

David was a prophet and a priest as well as being a king, and he had a greater revelation than others had in his day. He knew from God what to do, and he did it. David's people were blessed because the presence of God dwelt among them.

A Remnant of Flesh

Amos prophesied that God was going to restore His presence among His people. When He does, this is what will happen:

> **In that day will I raise up the tabernacle of David that is fallen, and close up the breaches thereof; and I will raise up his ruins, and I will build it as in the days of old:**
>
> **That they may possess the remnant of Edom, and of all the heathen, which are called by my name, saith the Lord that doeth this.**
>
> **Amos 9:11,12**

The people of Edom were the cousins of the Jews, because they were the descendants of Esau, Jacob's brother. Their Edomite kingdom was flourishing while Israel was still in bondage in Egypt, before the kingdom of Israel came into existence. But where is it today? You can't find it anywhere. It's gone.

It represents the kingdom of the flesh, whereas Israel represents the kingdom of the Spirit. Israel is in existence today, isn't it? It is the only nation that ever disappeared and was scattered all over the world, only to be reborn after two thousand years.

The Word of God works! God means what He says. Spiritual things last forever. Flesh represents temporal, changing things.

Have you ever seen carnal Christians? God is saying that He will reach into carnal churches and call out the remnant of those churches as the firstfruits. He says He is going to give us that group.

This the way He will do it: He calls us out of our bondage and prepares us to go back into the places we came from. After we are built up in the Word of God, God wants us to go save the lost and the heathen — even those in carnal churches who call themselves Christians but aren't. They don't know how to enter the kingdom of heaven.

God said He's going to cause us to get the vision for that group. He said, "I'm going to give you the remnant of Edom, and of all the heathen which are called by my name." (Remember, God said in Psalm 2:8, "Ask of me, and I shall give thee the heathen for thine inheritance....")

A Quick, Supernatural Harvest

Behold, the days come, saith the Lord, that the plowman shall overtake the reaper, and the treader of grapes him that soweth seed; and the mountains shall drop sweet wine, and all the hills shall melt.

Amos 9:13

We see here in Amos 9:13 that the man who is plowing for the next planting is going to be right on top of the man who is harvesting the last crop; "and the treader of grapes him that soweth seed." Here's a man sowing seed, and someone is processing the harvest right behind him.

This isn't a natural harvest, is it? This is a supernatural harvest Amos is talking about — the same harvest Joel prophesied of, when the former and the latter rains would come in the first month. In other words, the planting and the harvest are going to come close together.

The Holy Spirit will be responsible for these things happening through us. But we must be willing, prepared channels who will yield ourselves to God to reap this supernatural harvest.

Verse 13 concludes, "and the mountains shall drop sweet wine, and all the hills shall melt." These mountains are the kingdoms of this world. *Everything that has tried to keep men in bondage will be brought low.* God will reach into all kingdoms and take out of them the precious fruit of the earth.

That's what we are commissioned to do, and God said it will work. Nothing is going to prevent the work of the Church.

Verse 14:

> And I will bring again the captivity of my people of Israel, and they shall build the waste cities, and inhabit them; and they shall plant vineyards, and drink the wine thereof; they shall also make gardens, and eat the fruit of them.

No longer will God's people lose the harvest to a plague of insects or other calamities; they will reap the harvest, and its blessings will not cease, as we see in verse 15:

> And I will plant them upon their land, and they shall no more be pulled up out of their land which I have given them, saith the Lord thy God.

What does the land represent to us? *The land is symbolic of the Word of God.* It represents *provisions* God has made for us. When we enter into the Word and understand and act on it, we receive the provision of it. God has likened the Church's receiving this provision to Israel's taking the land that was theirs.

We, as the Church, are going to go take the land that is ours. God said when we do this, in the time of this great harvest, there will be no more being plucked up out of it. In the past, we have seen the Church repeatedly get in and out of the waves of revival. Wonderful things happened in those waves, and those revivals were necessary — I'm not criticizing anyone — but they came and went.

This revival is not going to stop! Hallelujah, it's here to stay! It's growing bigger and bigger and better and better. This wave is so big that the devil looks at it every day and says, "What am I going to do now?" He's trying to stop it, but he can't, because God has promised, "I will plant them upon their land, and they shall no more be pulled up out of their land which I have given them...."

This Is That

Studying the sixth seal of Revelation 6, we saw that great earthquakes accompanied Jesus' Crucifixion as well as His Resurrection, just as they did great acts of faith in the Old Testament. We saw that God literally shook the earth to signify that something earth-shaking was taking place. Then we saw the sun become black as sackcloth of hair and the moon become as blood, and we noted that these were not just natural happenings.

We will now return to Joel's prophecy to see further details:

> And it shall come to pass afterward, that I will pour out my spirit upon all flesh; and your sons and your daughters shall prophesy, your old men shall dream dreams, your young men shall see visions:
>
> And also upon the servants and upon the handmaids in those days will I pour out my spirit.
>
> And I will shew wonders in the heavens and in the earth, blood, and fire, and pillars of smoke.
>
> The sun shall be turned into darkness, and the moon into blood, before the great and the terrible day of the Lord come.
>
> Joel 2:28-31

I'm still having visions, and I'm going to keep on having visions until the Lord comes! Here in verse 28, Joel is explaining the dispensation of the Holy Spirit. Peter referred to this very prophecy on the Day of Pentecost, saying, "This is that." However, the Day of Pentecost only marked the *beginning* of this dispensation. We in our day do not have all of it, either; there's much more to come!

A great manifestation of the Holy Spirit remains to be poured out upon the earth.

In other words, because God will be pouring out His Spirit, and we will be responding obediently to Him, following on to know Him, He will be able to show wonders in the heavens and the earth — blood and fire and pillars of smoke. The sun shall be turned into darkness, and the moon into blood "before the great and the terrible day of the Lord come." This refers to a time before judgment — but it does not refer to the Great Tribulation.

Look at the beginning of verse 32: "And it shall come to pass, that whosoever shall call on the name of the Lord shall be delivered...." This, then, does not describe a time when men will run around looking for the Gospel, but they can't find it, as happened during the Dark Ages. This is a time when they *can* find it. It's a time when they're all hearing the Gospel and being challenged by the witness of God's signs and wonders.

Challenged by Signs and Wonders

One reason why we've never reached the whole earth is because we never went with all the power that God meant us to go with. When God confirms His Word with signs and wonders both in the heavens and the earth, it's a challenge to people. They've got to make a decision!

I heard the Gospel preached many times *before* I believed it, because I didn't *see* anything. In fact, I didn't see anything I wanted in the lives of the people who were preaching it to me. But when you see the confirmation of the Gospel — when it's right in front of your eyes — you've got to decide either, "Yes, that was God," or "No, that was not God," or possibly, "Yes, but I don't want Him!"

The manifestation of those signs and wonders caused you to come to the point that you had to make a decision. (Even if you decide that God is at work, but you don't want Him, your rejection of Him is still a decision.)

Let's say that in this future time, people will see someone's mutilated arm or leg be restored before their very eyes, or they see a man who has never walked get up and walk. At the same time, they are seeing signs and wonders in the heavens. Then when they hear the Gospel, they are required to make a decision.

God said He would do a quick work in the earth at the end of this age, and He is going to use signs and wonders to accomplish this. But we should have had them all along! God never intended for us to go tell people how to be saved *without* a powerful witness accompanying it to confirm His Word.

Thank God for everyone who has believed the Gospel — however they believed — but we must realize that God has ways of reaching people that we have just begun to comprehend! We're just on the edge of these things. God would have us reach the whole world! There are continents and entire nations that don't know Jesus yet.

How are we to accomplish this awesome task? Are we to knock on everyone's door? The Church has been doing door-to-door evangelism for decades, but that technique, good as it is, has not won the world. God means to reach the peoples of the whole world, and God *will* reach them all. And He shows us here in the Word how He is going to do it!

Chapter 9
Jews in the Age of Grace

And it shall come to pass, that whosoever shall call on the name of the Lord shall be delivered: for in mount Zion and in Jerusalem shall be deliverance, as the Lord hath said, and in the remnant whom the Lord shall call.

Joel 2:32

Joel prophesied that whoever would call upon the Name of the Lord would be saved, for there would be deliverance in Mount Zion and Jerusalem. That means that in the Church of the Lord Jesus Christ there would be deliverance for you, for me and, yes, eventually for Israel itself.

At the end of the age, God will use the Jews mightily to finish the work of preaching the Gospel here in the earth. They are "the remnant whom the Lord shall call."

To understand other future happenings, let us compare Joel 3:15 — which speaks of the time of the Great Tribulation, the time when judgment will come upon those who have rejected the truth — with a verse we have just seen, Joel 2:31.

Joel 3:15 says, "The sun and the moon shall be *darkened*, and the stars shall withdraw their shining." This must refer to a *natural happening;* something in the natural realm is causing the whole heaven to be darkened. How do we know this? Because, as we saw earlier, the moon simply reflects the sun.

But Joel 2:31 says, "The sun shall be turned into *darkness*, and the moon into *blood*, before the great and the terrible day of the Lord come." It is not natural for the moon to turn bright red when the sun is darkened. It means that something of a *supernatural* nature is happening here on earth.

This is exactly what Joel's prophecy is referring to: There is going to be a very great supernatural happening on earth before the end of this age! Remember, in Joel 2:30,31, the prophet told of wonders that would happen in the heavens and in the earth "before the great and the terrible day of the Lord come."

In other words, while the Church is finishing its work here in the earth, *"whosoever shall call on the name of the Lord shall be delivered"* (or saved). Whose name? The Name of the Lord Jesus Christ!

But millions don't know how to call upon Jesus of Nazareth now. In India alone, there are 600,000 little villages full of people, living in the most appalling circumstances, who have never heard of Jesus Christ.

Why should the Church in the West keep preaching the Gospel over and over again to the same people, when there are people in the developing nations who have never heard the Good News even once? That can't please God. God will reach all those people, and He will do it through the Church, so we need to get ready for this harvest.

Israel's Role in the Harvest

I heard a radio preacher say that it's too bad the Church won't be able to finish the work of preaching the Gospel; that it will take Israel to do what the Church should have done. Israel will have a part in this gathering of the harvest, but it will begin only after the Church *will have done* what God has told it to do. The reason Israel hasn't taken part in the harvest yet is because the Church hasn't finished its part yet.

In Romans 11, Paul is preaching about what will happen to Israel in the future. He starts by asking, "I say then, Hath God cast away his people? God forbid. . . .God hath not cast away his people which he foreknew. . . .Even so then at this present time also there is a remnant according to the election of grace" (vv. 1,2,5).

Which "present time" is Paul talking about? The first century, when he was writing his epistles. Even then, there was a remnant in the nation of Israel who believed and received Jesus Christ as the Messiah and looked for His Second Coming.

The rest of Israel, Paul said in verse 7, "were blinded." What blinds people? Their very religion can blind people to the truth. God has no favorite "religion." Religion is just religion to Him. Men must come to Him through His Son. He looks for men to worship Him in Spirit and in truth.

Furthermore, Paul continues, ". . .God hath given them the spirit of slumber, eyes that they should not see, and ears that they should not hear. . ." (v. 8).

Then he quotes David: "And David saith, Let their table be made a snare, and a trap, and a stumbling-block, and a recompence unto them."

The very Word that God gave the Jews — the table that they were to be saved by believing — became a snare to them, because they made a religion out of it. As Christians, we have done the same thing, haven't we? People who have practiced the Christian religion call themselves Christians. But they are not members of the real, living, vital Church. They've made a snare, a trap, and a stumbling block out of what God meant to bring deliverance and life.

God does not like religion! "Let their eyes be darkened, that they may not see, and bow down their back alway" (v. 10).

In the next verse, Paul asks, "I say then, Have they [the Jews] stumbled that they should fall? God forbid: but rather through their fall salvation is come unto the Gentiles, for to provoke them to jealousy."

There are now believers who are beginning to provoke the Jews to this spiritual jealousy to know God personally. God has sent some believers to live in Israel, where they are showing the Jews the love of God and interceding for them.

"Now if the fall of them [the Jews] be the riches of the world, and the diminishing of them the riches of the Gentiles; how much more their fulness?" (v. 12). When the Jews finally enter the New Covenant we are in, the world will enjoy even *greater* blessings from them than the great blessings the Jews have already given the world (Acts 3:25).

Starting with verse 15, Paul passionately makes the point, "For if the casting away of them be the reconciling of the world, what shall the receiving of them be, but life from the dead?"

Israel is not responsible for crucifying Jesus. The Jews are no more responsible than any other nation. Every nation was responsible for it. Every human being was responsible for it. But Israel was the nation that did it. (Only a remnant received Him.)

Consider this: If all the Jews had recognized Jesus and received Him as the Messiah, they would not have crucified Him. *But because they did, we have been reconciled to God!*

Israel in the New Covenant

Paul is saying, if the casting away of Israel brought about the reconciling of the world to Christ, what shall their receiving of Him as Messiah mean to Israel and the world? Hallelujah, God is going to bring Israel into the New Covenant.

God has no favorite nation — He loves all nations the same — but He has said certain things about Israel. His prophets have prophesied certain things concerning Israel, and what comes out of God's mouth always comes to pass just the way He said it.

The promises God made Israel will not come to pass just because of their religion, or because the Jews have pleased Him (if you look into their history, you will see they have not pleased God).

No, God is going to keep His promises to Israel *because He said they would come to pass!* Some will come to pass because the Church will, at long last, show the Jews something they want — thus provoking them to so much jealousy that they will accept Jesus as their Messiah and Savior.

> **For if the firstfruit be holy, the lump is also holy: and if the root be holy, so are the branches**
>
> **And if some of the branches be broken off, and thou, being a wild olive tree, wert graffed [grafted] in among them, and with them partakest of the root and fatness of the olive tree;**
>
> **Boast not against the branches. But if thou boast, thou bearest not the root, but the root thee.**
>
> **Thou wilt say then, The branches were broken off, that I might be graffed in.**

Well; because of unbelief they were broken off, and thou standest by faith.

Romans 11:16-20

Because of unbelief, the nation of Israel was broken off. The Old Covenant ended with Jesus' Crucifixion. The New Covenant in Christ's blood was extended to all. Those who received it were grafted into Christ. Those who rejected Him were broken off from their Old Covenant relationship with God.

In A.D. 70, when Jerusalem was destroyed by the Roman legions, that whole generation was scattered throughout the world, and since then they have been seeking God but not finding Him in their traditional religious practices.

Warning to Gentiles

"Thou standest by faith." How do we stand? How are we grafted in? How are we connected to the olive tree? By *faith* we have partaken of the fatness of the root. By *unbelief* the nation of Israel was broken off.

...Be not highminded, but fear:

For if God spared not the natural branches, take heed lest he also spare not thee.

Behold therefore the goodness and severity of God: on them which fell, severity; but toward thee, goodness, if thou continue in his goodness: otherwise thou also shalt be cut off.

And they also, if they abide not still in unbelief, shall be graffed in: for God is able to graff them in again.

Romans 11:20-23

What was the Jews' spiritual state when Paul wrote this? He says they were in unbelief. What are they still abiding in? Except for those who have individually believed in Jesus as their Messiah, they are still abiding in unbelief as concerns Jesus Christ. That's what God said. But if their unbelief turns to faith in Jesus, they shall be grafted back in, for God is able to graft them in again.

Paul continues to develop this theme in verse 24. Then he writes in verse 25:

> **For I would not, brethren, that ye should be ignorant of this mystery, lest ye should be wise in your own conceits; that blindness in part is happened to Israel, until the fulness of the Gentiles be come in.**

Paul doesn't want believers to be ignorant of this vital information about Israel. If any generation ever needed to understand Israel's future role clearly, it is our generation, because we will be the generation that helps bring these things to pass.

We need to be praying for the Jews, just as Daniel prayed for Israel's release from captivity. *Daniel brought it to pass through prayer, because he saw in Jeremiah's prophecies that it was the will of God.*

The Salvation of Israel

Who is God going to use to bring the saving of Israel to pass? *Today's Church, because we see that it is the will of God!* Who is going to bring the Jews into the New Covenant? We are, by believing God, by praying for the Jews' salvation, and by witnessing the love of God to them. This is how God is going to bring His plan to pass.

And if we see it in scripture, then we have a responsibility to pray, just as Daniel had. He didn't say, "Well, that's it! In seventy years, we're on our way back home." No, Daniel's response was to get on his knees and began to seek God toward that end.

Paul said that when the fullness of the Gentiles happens — when all the Gentiles who will be saved are saved — then the Jews will believe through the faith and love of those of us who have prepared the way for them.

We who cut up the fallow ground and plant good seed in it will cause the Jews to accept Jesus as their Messiah!

And so all Israel shall be saved: as it is written, There shall come out of Sion the Deliverer, and shall turn away ungodliness from Jacob:

For this is my covenant unto them, when I shall take away their sins.

As concerning the gospel, they are enemies for your sakes: but as touching the election, they are beloved for the fathers' sakes.

For the gifts and calling of God are without repentance.

Romans 11:26-29

Not every Jew is going to be saved; however, everyone who *believes* is going to be saved. How do we know that? From the ninth chapter of Romans, where Paul said a *remnant* will be saved.

Of course, the term "Israel" can mean more than just the natural descendants of Abraham. There are actually two lines that issue from Abraham: *spiritual* descendants and *natural* descendants.

Paul wrote of these spiritual descendants in Galatians 3:29: "And if ye be Christ's, then are ye Abraham's seed, and heirs according to the promise."

The Long-Suffering Character of God

Verse 29 of the above passage actually refers to the Jewish people, even though we Gentiles usually quote it as referring to us, the spiritual descendants.

116

Unfortunately, many of the natural line have died in unbelief, but a remnant shall be saved.

God's "calling" for Israel has never changed, even though He has had to discipline and judge the Jews along the way because of their unbelief. However, they will come into this New Covenant that we Gentiles live in! They will fulfill their part in God's redemptive plan for the ages after we have fulfilled ours — not because we have failed.

To summarize, God told Adam and Noah to populate the earth, and mankind has done this. God has not raised up this great population of 5 billion persons on earth for them to be lost and spend eternity separated from Him!

God has waited for this abundant harvest for years, through "plagues" of unbelief, sin, disobedience, distractions, and everything else that has "eaten" His harvest.

God has had long patience for the precious fruit of the earth, and He is willing to endure vessels that are fitted for destruction to gain those who are made for eternal life.

Now, at last, everything is in position in God's great redemptive plan — the "mystery" Paul referred to. Can you see that?

There are more people alive today than have ever lived on the earth until now. *God is going to have a harvest that will more than make up for what was lost in past centuries!*

Just how patient is God? Ask yourself how patient He is with you, and you will know! But just because God is long-suffering does not mean that He will delay judgment forever. He will not.

Chapter 10
The End of the Age of Grace

Once God has gathered all of the precious fruit (souls) of the earth unto Himself, *judgment will surely fall upon those who have rejected Jesus.* (All judgment is committed to Jesus, the Word of God, the Son of man, according to John 5:25-29.)

In Acts 3, we see Peter and John walking together into the Temple to pray. On the way, they healed the lame man at the Gate Beautiful. Peter preached a sermon that day to the people who came running, "greatly wondering" and amazed at this notable miracle. As a result of the lame man's healing, three thousand people got saved that day.

We, in this age, often go out and preach without *anyone* walking, leaping, or praising God. Yes, we get a few people saved — and God is pleased that they do — but do you see what He means for us to have: *God means for us to have multitudes saved — swept into the kingdom — as the result of signs and wonders!*

Peter preached:

> Repent ye therefore, and be converted, that your sins may be blotted out, when the times of refreshing shall come from the presence of the Lord;
>
> And he shall send Jesus Christ, which before was preached unto you:

> Whom the heaven must receive until the times of restitution of all things, which God hath spoken by the mouth of all his holy prophets since the world began.
>
> For Moses truly said unto the fathers, A prophet shall the Lord your God raise up unto you of your brethren, like unto me; him shall ye hear in all things whatsoever he shall say unto you.
>
> And it shall come to pass, that every soul, which will not hear that prophet, shall be destroyed from among the people.
>
> Yea, and all the prophets from Samuel and those that follow after, as many as have spoken, have likewise foretold of these days.
>
> **Acts 3:19-24**

Joel was one of God's prophets, so whatever Joel prophesied would happen before Jesus comes, will have to happen, won't it?

The Amplified Bible interprets verse 21 as, "Whom heaven must *receive [and retain]* until the time for the complete restoration of all that God spoke by the mouth of all His holy prophets for ages past. . . ."

Jesus is presently seated in heaven at the right hand of the Father. When Stephen was stoned, the heavens opened and Jesus stood at the right hand of the Father to receive him. So we know that He is there in His resurrected body, even while, by His Spirit, He lives in our hearts.

Heaven must receive and retain Jesus until "the times of restitution of all things, which God hath spoken by the mouth of all his holy prophets since the world began." *Everything that has ever been recorded in the Word concerning Jesus' Second Coming must come to pass exactly the way the prophets foretold it.* And everything that God has said the Church would have to do must come to pass exactly the way the prophets foretold it.

For example, if God said, "Go ye into all the world and preach the gospel to every creature," and Jesus came, leaving India in the mess it's in right now, His Word would have returned void! You see, Jesus can't return until we complete the harvesting assigned to the Church.

Why You Can't Predict the Lord's Return

Some Christians got all excited a few years ago, because they calculated from the birth of modern Israel in 1948 that Jesus was coming again in 1981. They took out big ads in newspapers, telling everyone to get ready, because Jesus was coming then. Well, He didn't.

The Word said that heaven would retain Jesus until everything that the prophets had said would come to pass.

If we could figure out just when *everything* would be fulfilled, we would know when He was returning, but that's not the will of God. *All such calculations are vain and fruitless.*

I've taught this truth for years, yet a few of my students have always gone out and "discovered" for themselves the date of the Lord's return! As a result, they got sidetracked, and their ministries suffered greatly.

Surely *everything* the prophets have said about Jesus' return was not yet fulfilled in 1981, was it? If those misguided people had understood that, they wouldn't have set any dates. (I'll guarantee you, they aren't making any more predictions!)

Getting off on such a tangent only detracts from the rest of the Gospel you preach.

We humans seem to have a fleshly desire to know exactly when Jesus' return will be. The Word of God, however, says that the angels do not know the day nor the hour (Matthew 24:36). *Not even the Son knows* — only the Father knows.

If Jesus doesn't know the date of His return, how could we know?

Peter mentioned "the times of restitution of all things" to the crowd that gathered when the lame man was healed (Acts 3:21). All that God meant for the Church to have is being restored to it: A complete restoration is under way. Wave after wave of revivals have come, but the restoration is not yet complete.

We need to get more and more into the supernatural. Kenneth E. Hagin says that we are on the edge of it right now. We need to listen to seasoned prophets of God. They won't misguide us. Some people think that God is suddenly going to raise up some unknown person with an amazing revelation about the future. I believe God is going to move through people with proven ministries — people who have a history of obeying and serving Him.

Listen to established, proven people, not to strangers who write about such things as hidden dangers of the rainbow, or of Christians being seduced in doctrine.

I read a little in one of those "expose" books until the author attacked numbers of well-respected ministers and stated that all of them were in error. He named three people whose doctrine was correct: the author himself, the fellow who helped him write his book, and one other man! (Does that tell you anything?)

Do you know who buys books like that? Baby Christians and those who don't know any better. We don't have to fight such attacks or even challenge false statements. We need to go preach the Gospel! Paul preached the Gospel. He knew it would straighten out people who were messed up.

Wading Into Revelation

Remember, end-time prophecy is not the *first* thing baby Christians need to learn. They need to learn who they are in Christ, get their minds renewed, and grow in the Lord. Then you can minister truths about prophecy to them.

I heard a story about a pastor who said to his flock, "Let's wade out into Revelation." They did, and he and half his flock drowned!

When I was first saved, I devoured all the books I could find about the anti-Christ, survival, the devil, and other tantalizing topics related to end-time prophecy. I read those books over and over again; I was fascinated by them. Do you know how much I grew in the Lord while I was studying all those things? Zero. Nothing. Those subjects do not build up the Body of Christ.

Blood and Fire

Joel prophesied that God will pour His Spirit upon all flesh. Also, the sun will be turned into darkness, and the moon into blood. But before the latter happens, God will show "wonders in the heavens and in the earth, *blood,* and *fire,* and *pillars of smoke*" (Joel 2:30).

As part of the outpouring of the Holy Spirit, God is going to show in the earth what *the blood* of Jesus Christ purchased for us! It's a "wonder"!

The blood of Jesus Christ speaks "better things than that of Abel" (Hebrews 12:24). It speaks life. It speaks deliverance. It speaks healing, health, safety, and preservation.

God is also going to show *fire* in the earth. Some people think this means some kind of natural disaster, but it doesn't. It's the fire of the Holy Spirit! John said of Jesus, ". . .he shall baptize you with the Holy Ghost and with *fire*" (Luke 3:16). Praise God, He'll fire us up!

This happened to a former Baptist minister who attended Rhema Bible Training Center some years ago. He and his wife had pastored for 50 years, and then retired to a comfortable little house in a Southern state. They bought two cemetery plots and two rocking chairs, sat down, and waited to die.

One day the Lord thundered, "GET UP OUT OF THAT ROCKING CHAIR!" The pastor asked hopefully, "Is this the day You are going to take us home, Lord?"

"No," the Lord replied. "I want you to go to Jacksonville, Florida. There's a man holding a crusade there. His name is Kenneth Hagin. I want you to hear him." So the couple drove to Jacksonville, heard Brother Hagin, and were filled with the Holy Spirit — and fire!

They got *refired*, attended Rhema, and went out in their own traveling ministry — and they were in their seventies! They were so grateful for the power of the Holy Spirit that now confirmed their ministry, for they had never experienced it before.

I was led into the baptism of the Holy Spirit by a Baptist chaplain in the service. After nineteen years in the ministry, he had cried out to God, "I haven't been able to help hardly anyone. If this is all there is, I want out of the ministry."

Within the week, someone bought hotel reservations for him and his wife to attend a charismatic retreat in Northern California. They were filled with the Holy Spirit and got *refired*.

In the next few months, 250 people on our Air Force base got saved and filled with the Holy Spirit: Protestants, Catholics, nothings, and everythings. I was one of them.

In fact, God moved the chaplain next door to me. As I would leave my house in the mornings, he'd be working in his front yard, and he'd look up and say, "Wasn't Paul great?" I'd reply, "Paul who?" He kept throwing out those little tidbits, and finally he got my attention, hallelujah!

What about the *pillars of smoke* Joel foretold — are they natural disasters? No, that's the glory of God in manifestation! There are references to it in the Old Testament.

Remember, the children of Israel were led through the wilderness by a cloud by day and *a pillar of fire* by night. Several references state that the tabernacle in the wilderness and the Temple were filled with smoke, which was the glory of God in visible manifestation.

Isaiah prophesied about the glory:

> Arise, shine; for thy light is come, and the glory of the Lord is risen upon thee.
>
> For, behold, the darkness shall cover the earth, and gross darkness the people: but the Lord shall arise upon thee, and his glory shall be seen upon thee.
>
> And the Gentiles shall come to thy light, and kings to the brightness of thy rising.
>
> Lift up thine eyes round about, and see: all they gather themselves together, they come to thee: thy sons shall come from far, and thy daughters shall be nursed at thy side.
>
> Then thou shalt see, and flow together, and thine heart shall fear, and be enlarged; because the abundance of the sea shall be converted unto thee, the forces of the Gentiles shall come unto thee.
>
> **Isaiah 60:1-5**

Notice in verse one that the glory is not just *in* you; it is *upon* you. We believers may not need to see it ourselves, but there are many people who do need to see it — and they need to see it on you!

I like to make the following confession based on these verses: "My light is come. I walk in the light, even as He is in the light. His blood cleanses me and makes me a vessel fit for the Master's use, so His glory can be seen upon me.

"Darkness shall cover the earth, and gross darkness the people, but the Lord shall arise upon me, and His glory shall be seen upon me. All shall come to me. O Lord, give me the heathen for my inheritance!"

You'll be amazed at what God will do for you in answer to this prayer! Just keep praying it. Oh, they'll come to you. They'll grow up with you.

Once we come into one accord and a unity of purpose, we will flow together, as Isaiah says in verse five. We have brothers and sisters in every part of this world with whom we need to be in agreement, in order to satisfy God's desire to seek and to save the lost. (Winning the lost, however, means more than ushering them into the kingdom; it also means teaching them everything Jesus has taught us.)

No Fish Story

Once we understand these principles in Isaiah 60:1-5, we will see the purpose of God for our life more and more clearly. "The abundance of the sea shall be converted unto thee" does not mean that fish are going to be converted! "Sea" is a symbolic word that refers to Gentiles.

What was prayed over Rebekah in Genesis 24, when she agreed to leave her homeland in Mesopotamia to become the bride of Isaac? ". . . be thou the mother of *thousands of millions. . .*" (v. 60). That's *billions!*

The present age is the only time in the history of the world when billions of persons could be converted! So now is the time when Isaiah's prophecy will be fulfilled!

126

So there will be a great manifestation showing what Jesus' blood has done. There will be a great manifestation of the fire of the Holy Spirit. And there will be a great manifestation of that pillar of smoke (the glory of God). In fact, these will be greater manifestations than we have ever seen in the earth!

Another reference to the glory of God is seen in Isaiah 6:

> In the year that king Uzziah died I saw also the Lord sitting upon a throne, high and lifted up, and his train filled the temple.
>
> Above it stood the seraphims: [a special category of angels] each one had six wings; with twain he covered his face, and with twain he covered his feet, and with twain he did fly.
>
> And one cried unto another, and said, Holy, holy, holy, is the Lord of hosts: the whole earth is full of his glory.
>
> And the posts of the door moved at the voice of him that cried, and the house was filled with smoke.
>
> **Isaiah 6:1-4**

The "train" that filled the temple is the glory of God that follows Him. The angel's statement, "The whole earth is full of his glory" is really prophecy, because it has never happened yet: The whole earth has not been full of the glory of God since Adam's time. Notice that "the house was filled with smoke." That, of course, was the glory of God in manifestation.

And that agrees with Joel's prophecy. Joel foretold wonders in the heavens and in the earth, blood, fire, and pillars of smoke.

God is already showing wonders in the heavens. Not too long ago, some Russians out in space reportedly saw a host of angels. The Russian government sent another team up, and they saw the angels, too. They said they saw huge angels of God out in space, and the angels were smiling like they knew some great secret.

They do! They know it's getting close to the Lord's return. We know this, too. We know we're living close to the end of time. We don't try to predict *when* this will be; we just know it *will be.*

This takes us back to the beginning of the Book of Revelation, where we saw that grace and peace were important to us. Knowing what God is doing in these end times, how well His plan is orchestrated, and who is in charge, gives us the freedom to see our part in God's plan and do what God has called us to do.

Let's look again at our background scripture from Revelation 6:12-14, describing the opening of the sixth seal.

> **And I beheld when he had opened the sixth seal, and, lo, there was a great earthquake; and the sun became black as sackcloth of hair, and the moon became as blood;**
>
> **And the stars of heaven fell unto the earth, even as a fig tree casteth her untimely figs, when she is shaken of a mighty wind.**
>
> **And the heaven departed as a scroll when it is rolled together; and every mountain and island were moved out of their places.**

Surely this is describing the Great Tribulation? No, not yet. *This passage shows us the effect of something that happens here on the earth.* In verse 12, we see that the sun is darkened, and the moon reflects *something other* than the sun: "the moon became as blood."

The Mystery of the Time Lapse

To understand this, we must go to Paul's teachings about what will happen *before* and *after* the coming of the Lord. For example, in First Corinthians 15, Paul said:

> **Behold, I shew you a mystery; We shall not all sleep, but we shall all be changed.**
>
> **In a moment, in the twinkling of an eye, at the last trump: for the trumpet shall sound, and the dead shall be raised incorruptible, and we shall be changed.**
>
> **1 Corinthians 15:51,52**

We will not all die: All of us who are living at the time of the coming of the Lord will be changed in the twinkling of an eye. Notice Paul didn't say we were going to *disappear* in the twinkling of an eye; he said we were going to be *changed* in the twinkling of an eye!

In First Thessalonians 4, Paul tells us something else about this change that will be experienced by the Church:

> **But I would not have you to be ignorant, brethren, concerning them which are asleep, that ye sorrow not, even as others which have no hope.**
>
> **For if we believe that Jesus died and rose again, even so them also which sleep in Jesus will God bring with him.**
>
> **1 Thessalonians 4:13,14**

The *spirit* and *soul* of those who "sleep" are presently with Jesus in heaven. When Jesus comes to catch the Church away, He will bring all those who have departed through the gateway of death with Him.

All who have died in Christ are going to come back with Him to receive a new, glorified body. They are coming back to the earth to receive that *body* because the *seed* of their old body is here in the earth!

For this we say unto you by the word of the Lord, [not by fancy calculations] **that we which are alive and remain unto the coming of the Lord shall not prevent** [the word is actually precede] **them which are asleep.**

1 Thessalonians 4:15

In other words, something is going to happen to those who have died and gone to heaven *before* it happens to us.

For the Lord himself shall descend from heaven with a shout, with the voice of the archangel, and with the trump of God: and the dead in Christ shall rise FIRST:

THEN we which are alive and remain shall be caught up together with them in the clouds to meet the Lord in the air: and so shall we ever be with the Lord.

Wherefore comfort one another with these words.

1 Thessalonians 4:16-18

If Paul stops to tell us what comes *first,* there must be some significance to the period of time between the two happenings. If these things were to happen instantaneously, why would he tell us which comes first? God doesn't waste words. If this had no meaning to us, Paul wouldn't state it this way. But it does have meaning for us!

Jesus is going to come to earth — not *on* it, but *to* it. And He's going to come with those who have died in Christ. They are going to receive their glorified body and be caught up with Him there in the clouds around the earth. (They come onto the earth; He never leaves the clouds.)

We who are alive on the earth have already been changed in the twinkling of an eye. We're still here on the earth, having been changed. But there is a significant time lapse until we are "caught up together with them in the clouds to meet the Lord in the air."

The Supernatural Grand Finale

What is going to happen during this time lapse?

Remember what Isaiah said would happen to the whole earth? *The whole earth will be full of God's glory!*

We read in Revelation 6: ". . .the sun became black as sackcloth of hair, and the moon became as blood; And the stars of heaven fell unto the earth. . . ."

Joel said the same thing. We read in Joel 2: "The sun shall be turned into darkness, and the moon into blood, *before the great and the terrible day of the Lord come.*" In other words, all of this will occur before the time of the Great Tribulation and judgment.

We saw in Joel 2:32 that *during this time before judgment, whosoever would call upon the name of the Lord would be saved.* Whosoever — anywhere in all the earth. That means that "whosoever" would need someone there to tell them how to get saved, because that is the usual way people are saved. Is God suddenly going to use some different way? No, He told the Church, "You go and tell them." We have been fulfilling the Great Commission ever since, and we will continue to fulfill it.

However, I believe there is going to be a grand finale — a very grand finale — a *supernatural grand finale* when the whole earth is filled with God's glory, and all flesh shall behold it together.

> **And the glory of the Lord shall be revealed, and all flesh shall see it together: for the mouth of the Lord hath spoken it.**
>
> **Isaiah 40:5**

That's a great manifestation of God in this earth. Jesus Himself will be there in the clouds, with the saints, surrounding the earth at that hour. I don't know how long this will last. I'm not trying to predict that — but I know it's a significant period of time, because God wouldn't have told us which event occurred first and which occurred second if it weren't.

Furthermore, I do not mean that there will not be any glory before this great manifestation. There will be a great deal of glory in manifestation, and it will be ever increasing until this finale, when *the last great testimony of the Church will be given to the world in a glorious manner;* especially to Israel, for, as we have seen, the Church has never yet provoked the Jews to jealousy.

I know one thing that will really provoke the Jews to jealousy will be when they see us caught away to be with their God! That is when they will finally realize that Jesus is their Messiah. That will be another thing that will provoke them to accept Him as their Messiah.

The Lamb Is the Light

There is a period of time in these prophecies where the sun is turned to darkness and the moon into blood. It is not dark *literally;* it is not the darkness that occurs when you turn a light out. It is dark by comparison to what is happening then on the earth!

Do you remember what Revelation 21:23 says about Jesus being the light of the New Jerusalem? "And the city had no need of the sun, neither of the moon, to shine in it: for the glory of God did lighten it, and *the Lamb is the light* thereof."

This does not say that there is no sun or moon in heaven; it says there is no need for them, because the Lamb is the Light of the city — His glory lights up the whole environment.

You see, when you are at the end of one age and the next age is just starting, an overlapping occurs. Some manifestations typical of the coming age start to occur during the closing days of the previous age.

An example of this happened when Jesus walked on the earth. Manifestations of God's glory that are typical of the Church Age — salvation, healing, and deliverance — were seen then. Jesus was beginning to show men in His day the same things that we see today. They had longed to see these things while He was still with them.

Now, even *before* the end of this Church Age — before we go on into the next glorious age — there will be manifestations of the greater glory that will appear when the whole earth will be filled with God's glory.

Some will conclude that these glorious manifestations will be part of the Millennium. No, what we are seeing here is what God will do to usher in the Millennium, thus completing His redemptive work here on the earth.

When you start teaching about supernatural end-time events, some people get the idea that you're "too far out." The prophecies we have been studying foretell supernatural events, don't they? What could the moon reflect that would make it look like blood? *The glory of God!* That's glorifying to Jesus, isn't it?

What is the moon going to reflect — the sun? No. It's going to reflect what is happening on the earth. *There will be a greater light here then, and the whole earth will behold this light, because all flesh will see His glory!*

All flesh will see this manifestation of the Gospel and, as Joel prophesied, whosoever shall call upon the name of the Lord shall be saved. At this time, the glorified Church on and around the earth will give its last great witness to this world and then be caught up together to be with the Lord in the air!

We saw in Revelation 6:13 that one of the results of the sixth seal being opened was: "the stars of heaven fell unto the earth, even as a fig tree casteth her untimely figs, when she is shaken of a mighty wind."

The stars of heaven symbolize angels. This does not have a literal meaning because, as we saw earlier, even the smallest star would destroy the earth if it fell to earth. (Angels are often referred to as stars in scripture.)

This refers to a great deal of angelic activity here on the earth — greater than ever before! Even in this day, we are seeing the beginning of the angels' increased activity.

Who commissions angels? Believers! The angels of God hearken to the voice of God's Word, we read in Psalm 103:20.

> **Bless the Lord, ye his angels, that excel in strength, that do his commandments, hearkening unto the voice of his word.**

Who is the voice of God's Word today? It's the Body of Christ here on the earth, isn't it? The angels are shaken onto the earth in great numbers, like figs falling off a tree, because of "a mighty wind."

What happened on the Day of Pentecost? "There came a sound from heaven as of *a rushing mighty wind*" (Acts 2:2). Praise God, that's the Holy Spirit. That's the Church manifesting the Holy Spirit in the earth, speaking and acting on the Word of God — and causing the increased activity of angelic beings.

These glorious activities are not necessarily limited to the future. We can enjoy them starting now and continuing through to the end of time. They will increase until we finish our work.

When you teach things like this, some people will look at you and say, "Well, the Church has been preaching the Gospel for two thousand years, and nothing like this has ever happened before." True, but that does not mean it won't. If God said it will happen, it will happen. Should we look at history, or should we believe the Word of God? Of course, we believe the Word of God.

The Wrath of the Lamb

Now let us look at what happens on the earth as soon as the Church is caught away and joins the Lord in the clouds:

> **And the heaven departed as a scroll when it is rolled together; and every mountain and island were moved out of their places.**
>
> **And the kings of the earth, and the great men, and the rich men, and the chief captains, and the mighty men, and every bondman, and every free man, hid themselves in the dens and in the rocks of the mountains;**
>
> **And said to the mountains and rocks, Fall on us, and hide us from the face of him that sitteth on the throne, and from the wrath of the Lamb:**
>
> **For the great day of his wrath is come; and who shall be able to stand?**
>
> **Revelation 6:14-17**

Here is the Church after it has finished its work. What is the scroll in verse 14? *The scroll symbolizes the kingdom of heaven departing from the earth!* Interestingly, Paul said to the Church, "Ye are our epistle written in our hearts, known and read of all men" (2 Corinthians 3:2).

To read a scroll, you must unroll it. But when it is rolled together, you can no longer read it, can you?

At present, the epistle of the Gentile Church is open and is being read by all men. The life you live and the words you speak are a testimony or epistle in the earth. But when everyone who can respond to you has heard the Gospel, you will have finished your work, and you will be caught away with the Gentile Church!

John refers to this catching away as a scroll being rolled together. SNAP! The scroll of the Church will be rolled up and disappear from the earth. What will happen when God catches the salt of the earth away? What will happen when the light of the world goes to be with Him?

Revelation 6:14 says that the next thing that happens is, "every mountain and island were moved out of their places." Does that refer to earthquakes or other natural catastrophes? No, in scripture *mountains frequently symbolize nations — large nations and kingdoms, or groups of nations that are banded together. Islands symbolize individual nations.*

In some texts, the word "mountain" even symbolizes the kingdom of heaven. For example, God said through the prophet Isaiah, "They shall not hurt nor destroy in all my holy mountain: for the earth shall be full of the knowledge of the Lord, as the waters cover the sea" (Isaiah 11:9). Here, the term "mountain" means God's Millennial kingdom, the whole earth.

The catching away of the Church will be such an earth-shaking event that every kingdom and nation in the world will be *shaken.*

The Church will leave the nations *plundered,* fulfilling the saying in Matthew 11:12, "the violent take it by force." This means that before they were caught away, Christians went out and boldly and aggressively removed from the nations every person who would come to God.

Can you imagine the effect it will have on those left behind on earth when several billion persons suddenly disappear? That will be earth-shaking. And when the light of the world is significantly extinguished, that will be earth-shaking, too!

When you take everything that is good out of a place, what is left? Only degeneration will remain once the salt of the earth is removed. What will it do? It will shake itself.

Imagine the effect on a town like Broken Arrow, Oklahoma, which has a large population of believers. Half the leaders of the community would be gone. So would a great segment of the population. Who is going to pay the mortgage? Who is going to make your car payment? Who is going to buy the groceries you've been buying? But this event is not going to shake only the economy; it's going to shake everything.

Everything that can be shaken will be shaken when the Church has finished its work and is caught away.

Verse 14 says, "the heaven departed as a scroll when it is rolled together." This does not mean the heaven of heavens, the atmosphere around the earth, or even the stars in the sky. It means everything connected with the kingdom of heaven that is being caught up from the earth to heaven.

What will continue to manifest the kingdom of heaven on earth? We will see in the next chapter of Revelation that the Holy Spirit will still be here, and God will still have a testimony here. This is not going to happen overnight, however; there will be a time of transition.

Bear in mind the incredible chaos that will exist in the nations when the entire Gentile Church departs. In Revelation 5 we saw gathered around God's throne redeemed from "out of every kindred, and tongue, and people, and nation." I'm convinced that at least half of the entire population of the earth will be caught away!

A Prophecy for Norway

Several years ago I was visiting in Norway. One day a man who happens to be a prophet of God accompanied me to that nation's equivalent of Independence Hall in Philadelphia — the building where Norway's founders declared it to be independent from Denmark and Sweden.

After we viewed the documents and pictures of the men who had been involved in that historic event, we walked around outside, praying. This man began to prophesy that salvation would come to more than two million of Norway's population of four million.

If God is going to do this in one nation, is He a respecter of persons? No! I have a tremendous sense of expectation regarding the size of the final harvest — that precious fruit of the earth. I'm not trying to predict numbers, but the harvest is going to be vast.

Let's not underestimate what God can do! And let's not underestimate what we will be able to achieve once God manifests Himself gloriously through His Church that has believed and done everything He told it to do. I believe that after the Church is glorified, there will be a last testimony to the world that will complete the Church's work. I believe this is clearly seen in the prophecies we have been studying.

The Shattering Effect on Those Left Behind

We have just seen that the departure of the Church will cause kingdoms and nations to be moved out of their places. Now, in Revelation 6:15, we have our first glimpse of the effect the Church's disappearance will have on the mighty men of the earth — the people who are left behind: "They hid themselves in the dens and in the rocks of the mountains."

Whenever there is a major crisis in the world, what do all the leaders do? They dive into deep holes in the ground — underground shelters — carved out of earth and rock. There are big holes burrowed in the ground all over this country and in most western nations. (The Soviet Union and Switzerland have extremely sophisticated and well-equipped underground civil defense shelters.)

We call our deep holes "command posts." In some cases, they are located in the sides of mountains. Whenever there is a crisis — for example, whenever things get tense between the Russians and this country — everyone of significance dives into his hole! That's where all the military leaders of nations operate from. In some cases, they are built far beneath the earth to survive nuclear attacks.

When I was in the Air Force, I used to work in one of these command posts. One day while we were having an exercise, I was reading my Bible in a command post in a midwestern state. I happened to read these verses describing people hiding themselves "in the rocks of the mountains."

"Lord help me — I'm in one of these holes!" I thought to myself. I could see that the way was already prepared for these things to come to pass. People are not going to have to start digging holes at the last minute; the holes are already there for them to jump into! Men who have rejected the truth — especially those in high places of authority — will hide in those places when these earth-shaking events begin to happen at the end of the age.

The exit of the Gentile Church will be the most earth-shaking event that the earth has ever seen!

Will There Be a Nuclear War?

People have asked me, "Do you think there will be a great nuclear war before all this happens?"

"Absolutely not," I tell them.

"Why are you so sure?"

I explain that if there were a massive loss of life on earth due to a nuclear war, where would God get His massive harvest of souls from? Multitudes are going to have to be *alive* on earth if God is going to have a great harvest. A general nuclear war would leave just a remnant of survivors — and perhaps not too many of them.

Some will be convinced that I'm going out on a limb by taking this position regarding future nuclear war. No, I'm just looking at what the Word says. If God said He's going to save a great multitude out of *every* nation, we couldn't afford to lose *any* nation. A multitude couldn't be saved out of a nation — any nation — if it were destroyed, could it?

"Well, He already saved them *before* the nuclear war happened," some people will argue.

That argument won't work, either. Look at some of nations this country is involved with, and you'll see that a great multitude has not yet been saved out of those nations. But God is working! He's working right now to get into the Soviet Union.

Graduates from Rhema Bible Training Center have been instrumental in translating and printing millions of Brother Hagin's books in the Russian language and then distributing them throughout the Soviet Union. To date, 2.3 million books — 100,000 copies of 23 titles

— have been taken behind the Iron Curtain in some very ingenious ways.

In addition, God is raising up a great number of people in Scandinavia who know that their ministry is to go into the Soviet Union and preach the Gospel. Some are already doing it. So God is reaching into the vast nation of Russia.

Some Thoughts on Gog and Magog

Much has been written about Ezekiel 38 and 39, which tell how Gog and Magog and their allies, including Libya and Persia, come down with them to attack Israel.

The tendency of many people after studying these chapters is to write those nations off, saying, "God's finished with them!" No, He's not, because God said He is going to take a people for Himself out of every nation, every tribe, every tongue, and every kindred. So before any of those things happen in Ezekiel 38 and 39, God will visit those nations first!

Yes, you can see how those nations are aligning themselves together and preparing themselves for what is going to happen eventually. But just because you see that, don't write them off. God can still reach a multitude of people in those nations.

There are people going around today trying to predict when Russia is going to invade Israel. That's just about as futile as predicting when Jesus will return. *Don't waste your time!*

God will do it, all right; the Word says He will do it. But I don't think it is going to happen before God reaches into those nations and takes out of them a people for Himself. That's His main concern, and that's our job.

God's harvest from the nations is how He is going to restore the years the locust, the cankerworm, the caterpillar, and the palmerworm have eaten.

If a great nuclear exchange occurred and half the harvest were destroyed by it, you would have another caterpillar plague, wouldn't you?

But God said He's going to *restore* the years that the plagues destroyed; He's going to restore the harvest that was lost!

Some Thoughts on the Great Tribulation

Jesus spoke of the Great Tribulation in Matthew 24:21. He said, "For then shall be great tribulation, such as was not since the beginning of the world to this time, no, nor ever shall be."

In other words, God's wrath will be poured out on unbelieving mankind — on those who have rejected the truth. Who can save them? By then, the day of both the Gentile Church and the 144,000 and their converts is past.

There isn't any answer. That's why we hear men crying to the mountains and the rocks in Revelation 6:16,17:

> ...Fall on us, and hide us from the face of him that sitteth on the throne, and from the wrath of the Lamb:
>
> For the great day of his wrath is come; and who shall be able to stand?

The answer is — no one. When that happens, there is no appeal. Mankind has gone to the end of the road. They have rejected everything that God has done to draw them to Himself — to save them — and now wrath will come upon them.

God's wrath, however, will not fall upon the world until it has first given up its precious fruit, and those souls have been gathered to safety in heaven.

We will explore this in greater detail when we examine what happens when the seventh seal of Revelation is opened. That information will be included in the third volume of this series.

Notes

Books By Brian McCallum:

Seven Letters to Seven Churches
Israel: God's Glory
Ministering Spirits Sent Forth
You and All Your House
As An Angel of Light
Day of the Lord

To order books and tapes by Brian McCallum,
or to contact him for speaking engagements,
please write to:

Brian McCallum Ministries
12645 East 127th Street South
Broken Arrow, OK 74011